**Architecture in Practice**

Mastering Architecture
Becoming a Creative Innovator in Practice

Published in Great Britain in 2005 by Wiley-Academy,
a division of John Wiley & Sons Ltd

Copyright © 2005 John Wiley & Sons Ltd, The Atrium,
Southern Gate, Chichester, West Sussex PO19 8SQ, England
Telephone (+44) 1243 779777

Email (for orders & customer service enquiries): cs-books@wiley.co.uk
Visit our Home Page on www.wileyeurope.com or www.wiley.com

Other Wiley Editorial Offices

John Wiley & Sons Inc., 111 River Street,
Hoboken, NJ 07030, USA

Jossey-Bass, 989 Market Street,
San Francisco, CA 94103-1741, USA

Wiley-VCH Verlag GmbH, Boschstr. 12,
D-69469 Weinheim, Germany

John Wiley & Sons Australia Ltd, 33 Park Road,
Milton, Queensland 4064, Australia

John Wiley & Sons (Asia) Pte Ltd, 2 Clementi Loop #02-01,
Jin Xing Distripark, Singapore 129809

John Wiley & Sons Canada Ltd, 22 Worcester Road,
Etobicoke, Ontario, Canada M9W 1L1

ISBN 0470092424

Cover: Minifie Nixon, Centre for Ideas, Victorian College
of the Arts, Melbourne, 2003 Photo © Peter Bennets

Series designer: Christian Küsters, CHK Design, London

Layout and prepress: Artmedia Press, London

Printed and bound in Italy by Conti Tipocolor

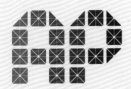

Architecture in Practice

Mastering Architecture
Becoming a Creative Innovator in Practice

Leon van Schaik

CONTENTS

6   **Introduction**
           Mastering Architecture
           Becoming a Creative Practitioner

           Zone 1
24   **The Individual in Mastery**
           The Natural History of the Creative Practitioner

           Case Studies
48   **Antwerp** Martine de Maeseneer
51   **Austin** Kevin Alter
52   **Brisbane** Donovan Hill
54   **Christchurch** Thom Craig
58   **Hobart** Leigh Woolley
60   **Kuala Lumpur** Architron
62   **London** Jenny Lowe
64   **Melbourne** Ian McDougall, Allan Powell, John Wardle
68   **New York** Michael Sorkin
72   **Perth** Geoff Warn
74   **Singapore** Look Boon Gee
76   **Singapore** Mok Wei Wei
78   **Singapore** Richard Hassell
82   **Sydney** Ian Moore, Stephen Varady, Durbach Block
88   **Scotland, Tokyo and London** Kathryn Findlay
90   **Ljubljana and Melbourne** Tom Kovac

           Zone 2
94   **The Groups in Mastering**

           Case Studies
           Self-Curating Collectives
110   Terroir
114   Iredale Pedersen Hook Architects
           Fostering Informal Associations
118   William Lim
120   Ken Yeang
           Partnerships for Life and Practice
124   Julian Feary and Katharine Heron – Enchaining Art
128   Vorberg and Kirchhofer – VK Architecture
           Migrating Contexts
132   Colin Fournier

136   Louis Kruger
         Establishing Poles
140   Sean Godsell
142   Allan Powell
         Firms That Sustain Innovation from Within
148   ARM
152   Lyons

Zone 3
156   **Thwarted Mastery**

Case Studies
164   Overshadowing
170   Technical Over-refinement
174   Forgetting Cultural Capital
176   Confusing the Knowledge Base
178   Failing to Elevate Innovations into a Metropolitan Discourse Rafael Moneo

Zone 4
182   **Encouraging Mastery and Innovation**

Case Studies
192   Collective Environments That Encourage
196   Regional and Provincial Environments That Encourage
204   Metropolitan Environments That Encourage

Zone 5
212   **Self-Curation as a Portal from Mastery to Creative Innovation**

Case Studies
220   Wood Marsh and Resistance
224   Leon van Schaik and the Ideogram Approach
228   The Melbourne Concourse of Architecture

234   Reflection
238   Useful Tips
239   Notes
243   Bibliography
244   Photo Credits
245   Index

Mastering Architecture

Becoming a Creative Practitioner

How to achieve mastery and convert it into a platform for creative innovation in architecture

Photomontage from the
series *Tall Tales (But True)*,
Peter Lyssiotis

Proposition

MASTERING A FIELD OF ENDEAVOUR PREPARES YOU TO BECOME A PRACTITIONER IN A FIELD. WHAT KIND OF MASTERY PREPARES YOU TO GO BEYOND THIS AND BECOME A CREATIVE INNOVATOR[1] IN THAT FIELD? IN THIS BOOK I DESCRIBE VARIOUS WAYS IN WHICH ARCHITECTS HAVE ESTABLISHED A MASTERY THAT HAS BECOME THE PLATFORM FOR THEIR PRACTICE AND THEN FOR THEIR CREATIVE CONTRIBUTION TO THE INTELLECTUAL DEVELOPMENT OF THE DOMAIN OF ARCHITECTURE. IN DOING THIS I DRAW ON OVER 30 YEARS – 40 IF I INCLUDE MY OWN EDUCATION – OF BEING AN ARCHITECT AND OF BECOMING INVOLVED IN THE EDUCATION OF ARCHITECTS, MUCH OF THIS EXPERIMENTAL IN NATURE. MY OWN INTERNATIONAL NETWORK OF COLLEAGUES, ESTABLISHED THROUGH MY STUDY AT THE ARCHITECTURAL ASSOCIATION (AA) SCHOOL OF ARCHITECTURE IN LONDON, AND MORE ESPECIALLY CREATED DURING MY PERIOD OF TEACHING THERE UNDER THE LEADERSHIP OF ALVIN BOYARSKY IN THE 1970S AND 1980S, PROVIDES THE CONTEXT FOR THE WORK WITH PRACTITIONERS THAT THIS BOOK'S PROPOSITION RESEARCHES AND REVEALS. MANY OF THE CASE STUDIES IN THE BOOK STEM FROM THIS NETWORK, AND THAT IN ITSELF IS AN EXAMPLE OF HOW GROUPS SUPPORT INDIVIDUALS IN THEIR REACHING TOWARDS MASTERY AND ON TO INNOVATION. WITHOUT THIS NETWORK I WOULD HAVE BEEN ILL-EQUIPPED FOR THE LATTER HALF OF THIS TIME, WHICH HAS BEEN FOCUSED ON WORKING WITH PRACTITIONERS WHO ARE ACKNOWLEDGED BY THEIR PEERS TO BE MASTERS IN ARCHITECTURE. THROUGH THEIR UNDERSTANDING OF THEIR MASTERY THEY HAVE BECOME INNOVATORS WHO ARE CHANGING THE WAYS IN WHICH WE THINK ABOUT ARCHITECTURE. I HAVE BEEN HELPING THEM TO INVESTIGATE THE NATURE OF THEIR MASTERY, AND WORKING WITH THEM WHILE THEY BUILD A CREATIVE AND INNOVATIVE DIRECTION FROM THAT UNDERSTANDING.

Origin of My Interest in Mastering Architecture

These architects have worked with me and with my team (Sand Helsel and Ranulph Glanville) in the 'by invitation' research programme at the Royal Melbourne Institute of Technology University (RMIT), henceforth referred to as a 'masters', in distinction from other programmes which are referred to as 'Masters'. I began this programme in 1987 because I could see that there was a broad but unacknowledged mastery in the work of practitioners who had been active for at least a decade,[2] but who felt themselves to be on the outskirts of debate, especially of international debate. I thought that bringing them into contact with each other within a reflective process might develop them personally, but also extend their confidence in the local discourse to the point at which they could argue for their work in any forum. They are invited on the basis of their having established – over at least a decade – a mastery of their domain and they are asked to reflect upon the nature of that mastery within a critical framework. Then they are asked to speculate, through looking at their ongoing work, about the future directions of their practice. Out of this, over and again, has arisen innovation. In the critical framework, we focus on their 'research question', the driving enquiry that motivates them, but which all too often has been submerged into background noise by the sheer demands of practice. A critical shift occurs when their reflection enables them to transcend their often almost compulsive worrying at the actualities of

Cities

The architects who are involved in this exploration of mastery and innovation come from many cities. Some now reside in Antwerp, Austin, Brisbane, Christchurch, Hobart, Hong Kong, London, Kuala Lumpur, Melbourne, New York, Perth (Western Australia), Singapore and Sydney. Some have lived in Tokyo. Many met as students in London; others were invited to participate in the research programme at RMIT that has provided so much of the material for this book. Their individual journeys and their supportive interactions with others are the evidence on which the propositions of this book rest. Over and again their stories reveal a consistent pattern of development as creative individuals. Over and again we see their successes playing out in accord with certain basic principles of engagement in any domain of knowledge and practice. Their mastery is forged in their experiences of city regions, and collectives that tend to network across more than one city support their innovations. City life is vital to mastery and to creative innovation. To know about the vibrancy of the intellectual life that a city region supports in a domain, we need to know how many fields that the domain sustains, providing ongoing attention to the good ideas of practitioners. Where a city is dominated by one position, architectural culture is weak. Where it is contested between two positions, it is robust. Where it is contested by three, it is vibrant. The stories of individuals, collectives and cities are interwoven in this account of achieving mastery and transcending it to become innovative and creative practitioners in many places.

their situation: a threshold between tribal repetition and innovation is crossed. Invariably they are surprised and elated by the command that this process gives them over their future practice. They report that being more aware of the nature of their mastery enables them to transcend it and to attract the clients who have similar interests. No longer are they trapped in generic public relations talk about the services they provide. They are different and they can demonstrate how and why. They come from around the world, mostly from the city-states of Australia – Melbourne, Sydney, Perth, Brisbane and Hobart – with a group from the Chinese diasporas in Singapore and Kuala Lumpur, and individuals from Christchurch, London, Tokyo, Hong Kong, Shanghai and New York. Conversations about the work have been extensive, with foci in Austin, Helsinki, London and Singapore. This is facilitated because architecture is an international practice and it is true to an extent that practitioners in a domain have more in common with each other than they do with members of their family who practise in other domains.[3]

What Is Mastery?

I began by defining mastery as a form of peer recognition. It seemed to me that people whose work had won awards, had been professionally reviewed in journals and had been the subject of monographs and exhibited in curated exhibitions were being acknowledged as having a mastery in a field of the domain of architecture. In the main such people have been working in the domain for a decade and they are ready to consolidate their position in a field and move into creative innovation. This, I have discovered, is a very common way of defining

Opposite Top
Charles Jencks, Diagram I – Critical Modernism; An Imminent Dialectic, Evolutionary Tree, 2000
This was developed while Jencks was teaching at the AA in the 1960s and was published in Charles Jencks, *Architecture 2000: Predictions and Methods, New Concepts of Architecture*, Studio Vista, London, 1971, p 46. It is interesting to review this seminal diagram in the light of 'the law of small numbers'. The notion that mastery is a local phenomenon, while innovation is necessarily projected into global discourse, makes this of critical moment. Jencks identifies six traditions in the domain of architecture: logical, idealist, self-conscious, intuitive, activist and unselfconscious. Within these traditions are the movements or 'fields' at play in any given era. In 1990, for example, neo-modernism, post-modernism, minimalism, corporate modernism, classical revivalism, biomorphic, deconstruction, ecstatic, CAD and internet are all at play. Further to this, Jencks suggests that the diagram needs to be more complex: 'it should be in three dimensions showing all the traditions simultaneously'. Even though there are large holes or tears in the two-dimensional diagram, the environment that this conjures up is counter to all of the evidence about intellectual change. I suspect that this is because what is lacking is not the third dimension but a cultural topography. The diagram suffers from a dislocation of place. This is similar to the way in which the conclusions Richard Florida draws from analysis of the cities of the USA become meaninglessly abstract when applied to the former nation-states of Europe. Apply 'place' to Jencks's diagram and the traditions at play at any given time shrink to no more than three.

Opposite Bottom
Leon van Schaik's Pictogram of today's Melbourne Architecture Community: Civics, Technics and Poetics

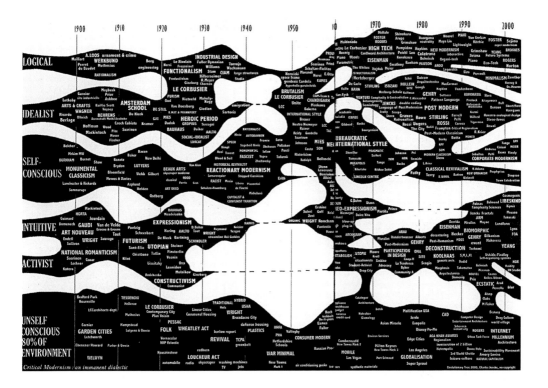

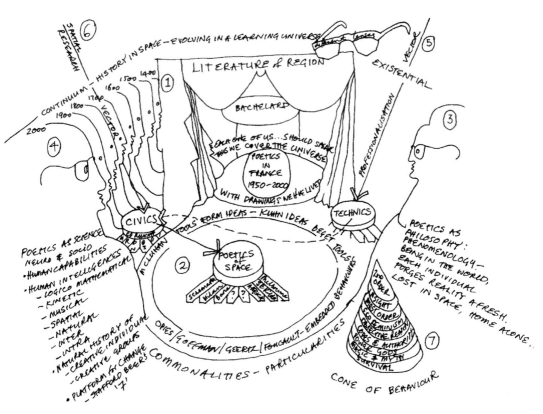

PROVINCE AND METROPOLIS

This cube reconciles three sets of conditions that are needed for creative innovation to occur

Cascading down the face of the cube which has the word 'INDIVIDUAL' inscribed on the top arris are the qualities of the natural history of creative individuals. Such people undertake a journey that begins on the fringes of a domain of knowledge: they are drawn to the centre, engaging for a formative period with peers who are undaunted explorers of the chosen terrain or field within the domain, where they find a problem that obsesses them. They become isolated through their sense of being on the verge of a breakthrough that they cannot quite explain. As they master the field they crave recognition but throughout their careers they maintain their marginality and exploit their awkwardness with existing structures as a source of the energy that drives them to transcend mastery and achieve innovation. Much of this takes place through 'weak' connecting – that ability to find linkages where conventional wisdom can see none. These characteristics have been identified by Howard Gardner through decades of studying creativity.

The arris between this face and the next is incised with the word 'REBELS'. Both faces have some of the qualities of the rebel and of rebellion identified by Albert Camus: to design is to assert an alternative future.

On the other face of the cube cascade the characteristics of the ritualised behaviours or social structures that support intellectual change. These structures have a public order but are not ossified into establishments. They often begin life as Salons des Refusés. These informal and often unconscious fields are subject to a 'law of small numbers'. Their members are intellectually enchained in small groups and divided by substantive differences into two or three positions. They thrive on competition and are motivated by ideas rather than material gains. These informal public orders encourage mastery and support creativity with the sustained attention that it needs in order to become innovation. Such public orders can thwart intellectual change by focusing on technical refinement, becoming the tools of an overshadowing personality, or by being complicit in the forgetting of cultural capital. Randall Collins, in his comprehensive survey of intellectual change, has identified these characteristics.

The top face of the cube is incised with 'ENVIRONMENT'. Here, between education and enterprise, and between the eidetic, subjective actuality of the province and the generalising abstracting discourse of the metropolis, these forces are played out in iterative achievements of plateaus of mastery and breakthroughs into innovations that demand new masteries. These processes are served by scholar-interpreters and calcified by curriculum definers.

Mastery is of the province, innovation is of the metropolis.

- SCHOLAR-INTERPRETERS
- NO CURRICULUM SYSTEM

- WEAK CONNECTIONS

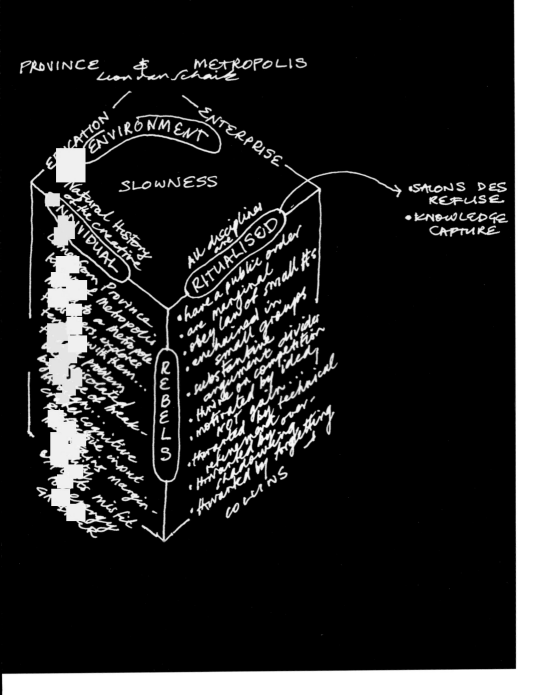

mastery. Howard Gardner gives just such an account from his more than 20-year research into the creative individual. Yet for him creative contributions follow mastery.[4] Robert Kegan defines mastery as culminating in that moment when you invent your own way, when you are no longer pursuing external patterns of behaviour and your 'pattern resides within', but paradoxically you are able to view your practice from outside.[5] Ernest L Boyer, who investigated the professoriate in the USA, came to the conclusion that in all the domains of scholarship, whatever the discipline or the intent (be it discovery, integration of new knowledge to existing, application of new knowledge to society's problems or dissemination and teaching), peer review was the way in which contributions were evaluated and validated.[6] I began by seeing this as a way in which mastery was recognised. It has become clear to me that mastery is a beginning, a platform from which creative contributions to a field within a domain can be launched.

Peer review is a persuasive, internationally recognised process. Most architects are aware of this need to engage with their peers, many wistfully so, because they feel that the pressures of practice preclude them from engaging in the ways that, deep down, they feel they should. They know that their progress from mastery to being creative practitioners depends on a reflective process, but there is no time. Some architects set aside an afternoon a week for personal research or organise weekly discussions in their offices. These are all symptoms of a need; but without a structure, without an understanding of the processes by which mastery is attained and then transcended, most of these events are transient and unsatisfying. Peer review needs to be taken more seriously as a process. In its heyday, the Spanish system included a peer-review of every architect's designs, in exchange for which clients' fees were paid up front into a trust fund and fees were disbursed through the peer-review process. Sadly, but perhaps understandably, these processes – even if preferably informal – need to be systematised if practitioners are to engage with them. The success of the RMIT programme lies precisely in the way in which it involves practitioners in a twice-yearly weekend conference in which they present their reflections to each other under the watchful eyes of critics from around the world and within a developing critical framework.[7] This framework is in itself a crucial body of knowledge, captured by the academics and published so that it can develop and not simply be a cycle of recurring arguments. Peer review must be structured and related to theory and research if it is to be effective.

Behind all this lies the question of who benefits from mastery and the creative innovation that can flow from it. As Boyer argued in his study of architectural schools in the USA, it is the belief that this practice delivers social benefits that gives it its driving power. As Theodore Zeldin has so exhaustively observed, whether our means of transport to an evolution of awareness is 'to obey' (but which god?), or 'to negotiate' and bargain (but what if we lose?), or to 'cultivate one's own garden' (but who will share it?), or 'to search for knowledge' (but to what end?), or 'to talk' (but who listens?), or 'to be creative' (but for whom?), the overriding aim is to meet others and to link with them.[8]

Is Mastery International?

While it has been studied by scholars on all continents, mastery is not, however, an international currency. What passes for mastery in one city can look suspiciously empty to the practitioners from another city, even when they are at first impressed. The emperor's new clothes are at first difficult to see and then suddenly very easy to see. Too easy. A fascinating example of this lies in the fate of a collection of Australian art made by a Texan who had become enthralled by the way in which Australian artists had engaged with the ideas at large in 20th-century art. When he died, his collection was sent back to Australia to be sold: no Texan institution could 'see' the mastery that it contained. In a world dominated by nation-state consciousness, the work seemed provincial and derivative – after all, anything that matters has been done first in the metropolis of our own supreme state! In this way, mastery in one context is dismissed, much as were Russian claims to the invention of the steam engine or the belief that Logie Baird invented modern TV or that Turing was the inventor of the modern computer. These claims have currency only in the country – or the community – in which they are made. Every innovator is on a journey from the province of their subjective actualities to the metropolis of self-conscious critique and back again in a forward-moving growth spiral.[9] Mastery on its own tends to be frozen in a repetition of at best tribal verities. Innovation, we now know, is confirmed in the best and most widely cast discourse on a field within a domain.

Morphic Resonance

A positive effect of globalisation is that increasingly we can acknowledge that ideas well up all over the world at about the same time. What is of interest is how people develop them and what is done with them, rather than who was 'first'. Nation-states are on the wane as cultural condensers and we are less likely to argue that our particular group 'invented' the steam engine. The notion of morphic resonance[10] has increasing support. We can acknowledge that what is interesting is how individuals in different cultures – usually city regions[11] – deal differently with the same emerging ideas. What remains internationally exciting, and necessarily so, is the validation of innovations built on mastery: the creative change effected by individuals who build on the platforms of their mastery to extend our understanding of what the domain itself is about and what it can accomplish.

Innovation – The Need to Transcend Mastery

Why, if mastery is increasingly something that we can accept as having regional and provincial boundaries or frameworks, is innovation not similarly bounded? Well, it can be, but only at the risk of special pleadings that historically have always led to tyrannies and bad science. Bad science is untested science, and all too often that has proved to be corrupted science – science in which data is manipulated to support the power of certain individuals. This matters in architecture too: the health of all scholarship depends on the quality of the peer review to which it is subjected.[12] While the views of the tribe are very relevant to describing the conditions in which local mastery is forged, the quality of innovation is tested against all innovations in a field and in an international arena. There are hopeful signs that this arena itself is also changing, as the background frame for practice shifts from the 19th-century paradigm of the 'professional' to the more current paradigm of the 'researcher', and that it is thus less controlled by the old (imperial) metropolitan hierarchies. Perhaps that is just a hope, but not a vain one. The practice of Ken Yeang is a clear example of a research-led practice in my generation and more and more contemporary architects are operating in this way – brought together in Archilab, the current international, experimental architecture peer-review forum.

Two Levels – Mastery and Innovation

This book operates on two levels, then: one level deals with the conditions for the forging of mastery of a kind that gives rise to platforms for creative development in design; the other level describes how some architects have used a platform to become innovators. Clearly I need to show that the arguments about how you achieve mastery are about an expertise that is more than simply replicating what already exists – even undergraduate schools of architecture have ambitions well beyond that. I must acknowledge here that there is a strong school of thought that would challenge this view, arguing that restless innovation is precisely what has brought architecture into disrepute. These traditionalists, such as Kenneth Frampton, have some interesting arguments that I will address, but I have to state that I see no way back (to the pre-modern vernacular state), only ways forward.

These levels, therefore, are intertwined and I will adduce innovations to show how platforms of mastery lead to creative development. In the book I marshal my evidence in five zones.

Zone One – The Natural History of the Creative Practitioner

The first zone dwells on the natural history of the creative practitioner, drawing on the individual accounts of practitioners who have submitted their investigations into their mastery to my guidance[13] and to the full glare of the scrutiny of their peers. While developing mastery in a domain is important, and this section gives guidelines based on what is known about how this is done by individuals, the crucial issue is how individuals transcend their mastery and become creative innovators in practice. Although this book gives clear guidelines on how you might internally develop your own work, it also argues for a very necessary wider engagement, and three out five sections deal with this broader engagement or context. In this zone, however, I examine the first steps by which individuals situate themselves in the dynamic between the province that they inhabit subjectively and the metropolis they aspire to influence consciously. I look at: how this is usually driven[14] by some 'physical, psychic or social obstacle' that makes the person feel 'marginal'; how this influences the selection of the metropolis into which they will project their discoveries for validation, which is an individual, but – as we shall see – crucial matter, because failure to so curate yourself dissipates the energy that should be coming from appropriate 'sustained attention' to innovative initiatives; how individual development depends on selecting a supporting group of peers who are comfortable with taking chances and determined to succeed;[15] how creative individuals find the problem area that becomes the focus of their creativity; how they deal with the isolation that choosing an area of operation induces and find ways to describe to the community at large the nature of the breakthrough that motivates their (re)search; how they learn to derive energy from their pre-existing sense of being on the edge; and how through their creative careers they sustain that energy by maintaining a resistance against incorporation into an established or brand-determined role.

The natural history of the creative individual.

The ritualised behaviour that supports intellectual change or innovation.

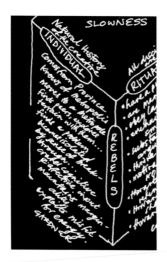

Zone Two – Peer-Group Support for Mastery and Innovation

The second zone examines the role of peer groups in establishing platforms of mastery that support innovation; how would-be innovators are helped by finding a group of peers who are willing to experiment, fail and start again; and how these groups are often clustered around mentors. This draws on a wider set of experiences, including my readings of the experimental years at Black Mountain College in North Carolina,[16] which supported the emergence of the painter Robert Rauschenberg's extraordinary assemblages of media as well as the music of John Cage and the dance of Merce Cunningham. It also draws on my direct experience of the Architectural Association School of Architecture in its 1960s golden age, and then on reflections on my own venture in establishing a research-based culture in design education at RMIT. Here I look into the importance of rituals of social activity in defining and establishing mastery. I argue that the rituals of the 'professional' are no longer helpful and that those of the 'researcher' are increasingly those adopted by successful creative practitioners. The importance of mentors and mentoring, the enchainment of generations in the pursuit of innovations or in denial of them are crucial areas of evidence about the nature of mastery, as is the phenomenon of 'the law of small numbers',[17] which explains why any generation of creative practitioners in a domain pursues more than one, but probably no more than three distinctive fields of innovation. I discuss the vital roles of certain kinds of competition that concern ideas rather than gain and pursue substantive differences rather than trivial technicalities. I argue that these group functions are essential to innovation, which arises when individuals use a platform of mastery to define a creative development that is then subjected to sustained attention by an ever-widening circle of people.

Zone Three – Thwarted Mastery

The third zone looks at the conditions that thwart the development of innovation from mastery. These arise when a community forgets its cultural capital, and here I suggest that this includes governing and commissioning elites, at any level in a community, who forget what architecture can and should provide. Innovation is also thwarted when architects forget what their own province has achieved and fall completely under the sway of international practice without a provincial component. 'Look! I can do that too!' is not a useful battle cry. Thwarting conditions arise when powerful individuals overshadow a domain, using their position to dominate the terms of discussion, the engines of patronage and the lines of communication. They also arise when a community of peers itself forgets the larger picture and focuses debate on technical over-refinement within a narrow, usually tribal definition of mastery. Thwarting also happens when a domain focuses its energy on a wrongly or poorly defined knowledge base, trying to exclude others rather than include them.

Zone Four – Promoting Innovation

The fourth zone examines conditions that actively promote the emergence of creative developments from platforms of mastery. There are ways in which we can manage our personal environments so that they encourage innovation; there are regional and provincial environments that encourage mastery; and there are metropolitan conditions that promote innovation. Here I explore our relationships with educational events that support the development of mastery as a platform for innovation, places like Black Mountain College, the Architectural Association School of Architecture in the 1970s and 1980s, RMIT in the 1990s and currently. Here I will draw on examples of the supportive patronage of architects, looking at, for instance, the Kumamoto Artpolis, Canalhead in Peckham, the Jubilee Line and the city of Groningen, which systematically provided opportunities for innovations to be tested through their realisation within an urban development strategy. I will also reflect on my own experience in developing a patronage system at RMIT, a system that has sought to give a voice to the three fields of innovation in architecture that are flourishing in Melbourne today. And I will examine some theoretical stances that promote the metropolitan embrace of innovation – theories like 'terrain vague', 'mobile ground' and 'parafunctional space'.

Enchainment diagram
All of us work with or against our peers in our own generation, with or against our mentors in previous generations, with or against our students or colleagues in the coming generation. To be aware of the way we position ourselves is to use the energy devoted to this field of influence well.

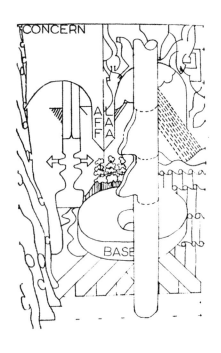

Zone Five – Self-Curation

Here I explore some personal strategies that people use, or could use, to position themselves to win energy from the environments that they encounter and those that they need to create on their journeys towards mastery. This extends through mastery's many possible confirmations as a platform for innovation and through the processes of securing the sustained (metropolitan) attention that turns creative breakthroughs into innovations. This is a reflective process, which when properly understood can be managed as a process of 'self-curation'. Becoming a curator of yourself is a way of: knowing how to handle yourself at each stage of your journey as an individual creative person; locating yourself in the supportive and challenging environments that forge mastery; finding those peers who help you to transform mastery into a platform for intellectual change; and seeking out those situations that clarify your creative breakthrough into innovation. I conclude with a mental model of a concourse on which the various aspects of this process can be visualised in dynamic interaction.

Case Studies

The zones are illustrated with examples of architecture from the case studies that I use to illuminate them, and here I acknowledge the difficulties of representing the essentially spatial practice of architecture with photographs and verbal descriptions. This is especially true as it is central to my argument that there is not one clear definition of what is 'right' architecture. Also, when a domain such as architecture is vibrantly involved in the processes of intellectual change, it will be divided into two or three distinctively different fields. Much of what architecture does cannot be communicated through two-dimensional images alone. Superficial similarities leap to the eye and are created through our internal pattern-making processes. These likenesses are pitfalls and lead architects into assumptions that thwart their understanding of what needs to be done. I defer to Steen Eiler Rasmussen's wonderful catalogue[18] of the qualities of architecture, its texture, colour, rhythm, etc, but also to a proposition about why architecture matters at all. We, as children, learn to negotiate our world using common capabilities that engage us in all of these terms, and every human embeds architectural knowledge. It is my view – shared, I think, with Rasmussen – that it is the practitioner's role to develop designs that, when realised, reawaken that basic interior knowledge of architecture and its best qualities in us all. However, in claiming that such practice provides environments that sustain us in a more than functional manner, I acknowledge my own adherence to one of many propositions about the nature of architecture. As we now know, these common spatial capabilities unfold in distinctive environments that give them specific colourings – like languages – and even in each such shared mental space, two or three substantively different propositions about spatial knowledge will be at play.

These case studies are accounts developed through conversations with their subjects.[19] They are stories that enable their tellers and that, taken together, help those who read them find their own paths.[20] They are stories that sketch ways in which different people have established their mastery platforms and transcended them through innovations that have the capacity to change the way in which we think about the domain of architecture.

Groningen, Kumamoto and the Jubilee Line

These are examples of city regions that have used their patronage of public works as a way of supporting innovative design. One of them (the town of Groningen, Holland, top two images) has raised levels of public awareness and interest, but has not played into the support processes that sustain communities of practice locally. One of them (Kumamoto, Japan, lower image, left) has directed its patronage to support emerging architects from its country. The other (Jubilee Line, lower image, right) has played a part in establishing London as a city that sustains local innovation.

At Groningen the interest in design has been the focus of a museum approach. Noteworthy design is collected and displayed inside a design museum. Buildings by internationally branded architects are also collected through the public works programme. Notable amongst these is the museum itself by Bellini. Groningen has become a tourist destination for designers, but it has not developed the vibrant design community that Antwerp to the south has created. Kumamoto Prefecture has for three decades used its public works programme in an 'acupuncture' social programme, focusing first on heritage projects and then on two waves of infrastructure building, from bridges to fire stations to puppetry workshops and theatres. Young Japan-based architects have been given all of this work and many have become internationally renowned as innovators. Roland Paoletti used his commissioning role on the Jubilee line to create a series of stations by London architects – many of whom were better known for their work outside the city. His linking of the work of Michael Hopkins (Westminster), Ian Ritchie (Bermondsey), Ron Heron (Canada Water), Norman Foster (Canary Wharf), Will Alsop (North Greenwich) and Chris Wilkinson (Stratford) has transformed London's reputation for sustaining communities of innovative practice.

The Individual in Mastery

The Natural History of the Creative Practitioner

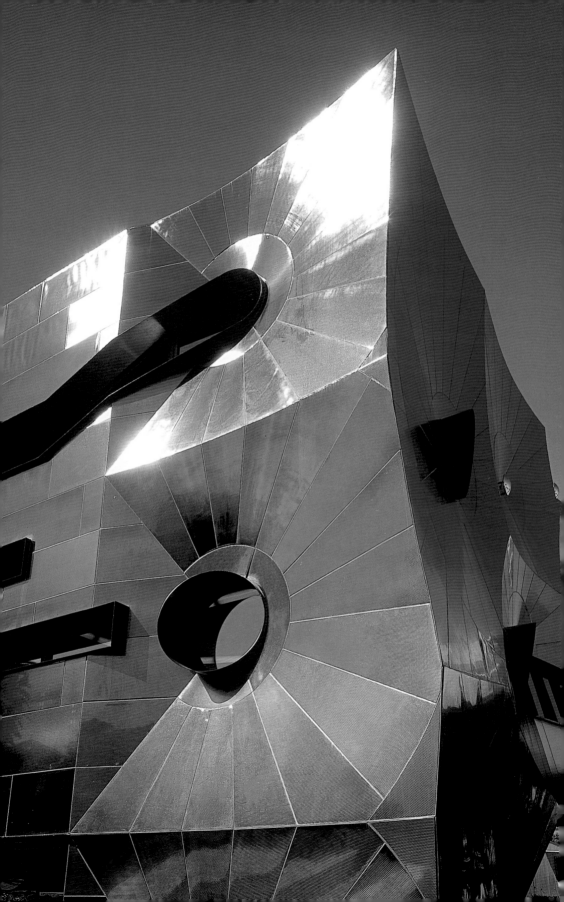

Mastering the Status Quo or Mastering Architecture?

The people I have worked with, and whose histories I draw on, all aspire to something more than the mastery of architecture. They want to make a contribution to the architecture's development, not simply to replicate current good practice. This ambition is the essential motivator for any pursuit of mastery. Yet there are those who see such ambitions as treacherous, believing that some absolute plateau of accomplishment can be reached, and that it is traitorous to abandon this in the pursuit of what they see as spurious, individualistic originality. For some, such as Roger Scruton and HRH Prince Charles, that plateau was the Georgian period, while for others it is the white architecture of high modernism. Curiously, all of these critics believe that their own area of scholarship is exempt from this classicising process. Guy Rundle[21] describes how government, through planning, fails to engage with creative innovation, while its funding in other areas supports it – critics may even assert that such invention is appropriate to music or theatre, but not to architecture. In doing this they unconsciously point to the huge importance of architecture to our wellbeing. It is too dangerous to be left to the specialists, they aver, citing this or that urban disfigurement. What they fail to discern is that the vast majority of these failures lie outside the realm of architectural endeavour, as indeed most attempts at music-making fall short of captivating. You cannot make architecture a special case. What we need is not aspic but a healthy process and a wide understanding of that process and its workings. I believe that architecture is as much driven by human curiosity as are science and art, and that these attempts to freeze it in the image of a preferred period are misguided and doomed. People seek to master a domain in order to contribute to its development, and architecture is no different from music or poetry in this. Of course, some experiments will result in work that is less popular – like 12-tone music. However, there is no lively area of human activity that is exempt from the drive to push the limits of understanding and experience further. Even those who conceive of themselves as following in the footsteps of a master, Georgian or modern, find that in order to copy they have to invent – or what they produce falls far below the excellence that the masters of the past

Mastering Architecture

Mastering the Status Quo

There is a strongly held position that innovation in architecture is always a betrayal of its relationship to communities at large. This single-ontology argument sees perfection being evolved over aeons of time from a primitive hut into the temple form perfected by the ancient Greeks. Certainly exemplars exist, as theatrically manipulated as the chapels of the Lutheran cathedral in Helsinki (top) or as unselfconscious as a summerhouse on a nearby waterway (above). However, as Raymond Erith's work shows (left, three images), mastery awaits innovation even within a position that asserts that it is the one true path.

Previous spread
Minifie Nixon, Centre for Ideas, Victorian College of the Arts, Melbourne, 2003

achieved when they were themselves pushing the limits of what was possible. Raymond Erith's enduring works are not the pastiche Georgian villas that, like Quinlan Terry's works, seem somehow to have failed to grasp the easy manners of their exemplars, but, rather, they are the curious pavilions in the villas' grounds which are strangely evocative and unique amalgams of rural forms. And while the New York Five[22] demonstrated their dexterity as modernists in that famous suite of houses, what came next in their careers was the attempt to make individual contributions to architecture through very divergent researches. So I think we need to accept that establishing a mastery is only a first step for an architect. It is on that first-step mastery and its nature that I am focused in this chapter.

Province and Metropolis

How do the architects I have studied first establish a platform of mastery from which to launch their individual researches? They begin by being onlookers, observing the field from a peripheral position. They are intensely aware of what is going on, and attempt to join in, but find themselves uncomfortable within any particular school of thought. Some approach architecture from other scholarship areas, only studying formally when they find that architecture has become an all-involving obsession. Minifie Nixon approached architecture from the vantage point of medical and computer studies. This trial-and-error approach seems a natural one for any student of architecture, although only a few schools allow for this in their curricular structures. The Beaux-Arts

Right top three images
Peter Zumthor, St Benedict, Somvix, Switzerland, 1989

Right bottom three images
Sean Godsell, Carter Tucker House, Victoria, Australia, 2000
Peter Zumthor's work has assumed some of the character of cliché in that elements have become part of a new lingua franca in neo-modern architecture. His example as a mentor is more profound than that, however, and it is no accident that the geographical spread of his practice is relatively confined to northern Switzerland and adjacent territories. His modernism is deeply inflected with the provincial actualities of sites. This little shingle chapel, St Benedict in Somvix, replaces one that was lost to an avalanche. Its form has everything to do with the specificity of its situation, as does its carefully conceived carpentry detailing. Sean Godsell's work is also single-mindedly tailored to its sites and the needs of clients. This dune house, the Carter Tucker House, is a lock-away holiday retreat and intensive work studio for its owner, an internationally travelling photographer. Where the chapel is closely sealed against the elements, the house admits light and air in widely nuanced modes. Zumthor has proved to be a mentor who opens people to the actualities of their situation.

view of the classical problems of architecture – symmetry, axiality and decoration – which is still espoused even by the innovator Greg Lynn (who in so doing, as I will argue later, risks thwarting his innovations by tying them back to past thought-systems), dominates, even if not literally, educational thinking. The success of Alvin Boyarsky's 'there will be no curriculum system!' approach at the Architectural Association has been observed more than it has been replicated. Innovative architects may emerge from either educational system, however, some in revolt, others nurtured. But this wary, peripheral observer stance continues well after graduation for the architects I am considering here. It is as if one of the strategies that they have mastered is that of being able to observe the field from a peripheral position, rather than being locked into a received wisdom or an established school. Perhaps this is why so few large firms have succeeded in maintaining hothouses of innovation in their midst. Corporate governance too readily lapses into a desire to control a corporate style, and that drives out the uneasy scepticism of people who are on a track to innovation. I don't think this is insurmountable, and there are many instances of moments when large firms (such as Arup) have supported innovation, usually when they acknowledge the need for a Research and Development section with its own culture. However, in the main innovators seek out different, more flexible and usually small support structures. These architects maintain and jealously guard a 'province' of endeavour that they test only periodically in the crucibles of the contemporary metropolitan condition: exhibitions, publications and competitions. Some, like Wood Marsh, go to considerable lengths to keep their province obscure, insisting on the inefficacy of words for articulating their architectural visions and using exhibitions to tease people into a realisation of what they hold important in design. However they do it, they have in common a strong commitment to provincial experience – the source of actuality – and an equally determined desire to relate this experience to a general or metropolitan discourse.

Left
Edmond and Corrigan,
Ringwood Library,
Melbourne, 1994
Much of E+C's work uses the graceful organic forms of Alvar Aalto conflicted with Brutalist energy. These influences inform an ideological position that owes a great deal to a humanist acceptance of the city as it is wrought by people: imperfect and imperfectable; yet always, through manifesting the dreams of all, these are 'Cities of Hope'. There is a resonance with the interest in what has come to be a city's narrative that Venturi and Scott Brown displayed in *Learning from Las Vegas*. While Corrigan's planning has the almost fatalist acceptance of error at its core, there is a consistent kindness to people in the interior detailing that owes much to the exemplar of Aalto. While his influence on Edmond and Corrigan's work may not seem obvious, the Ringwood Library uses many of the Finnish architect's profiles in its section, profiles he often used on plan. Aalto's mentorship is open-ended: he once argued that in campus planning it was essential not to complete the design, so as to leave space for the work of architects to come.

Above left
From Carey Lyon masters,
Towards a Brand New City,
Transfiguring Ordinary, RMIT,
Melbourne, 1995

Above right
Carey Lyon, Botany North
Extension, Melbourne
University, Melbourne, 2004

In the work of this firm, the engagement with Robert Venturi has taken a very different turn. Arguing that the room for architecture has become confined to a very small zone on the surface of buildings, Lyons have discovered the possibilities of working the skin from inside and out, creating an internal facade as well as an external one. This has turned out extremely well for their clients, who are mainly service providers in health and training. The difference between Lyons and E&C points to what characterises Venturi and Scott Brown as mentors: they do not prescribe; they note and wonder about implications, so opening up options for generations to come.

Peers

What is the purpose of this positioning on the periphery? It seems to be twofold. The first function is to establish a network of peers who have similar interests, not only in kind but also in intensity. These networks are often fairly tribal in the sense that they are geographically confined, usually to a city and its region, and generationally defined as groups cluster around some selected mentors and/or texts. They have often been gender-defined as well. They seem to be concerned with the ownership of local cultural capital. I will deal with these clusterings in more depth in Zone Two. In this chapter the focus is on the individual and the path taken by individuals as they establish a platform of mastery that is a launch pad into creativity. So it is important to note here that individuals who become successful creators are not satisfied with the tribal group as a context.

Mentors

They seek out mentors all over the world – Corrigan and Aalto, Venturi and Rudolph, Lyon and Venturi, Godsell and Zumthor, etc. Sometimes these relationships are based on actual meetings, often they are remote but enduring admirations leading to intense study and attempts at replications. It is important to note that some mentors are more fruitful than others – Frank Lloyd Wright's exemplars have proved to be a dead end, and people who picked Louis Kahn as their mentor have seldom escaped from his clutches to become innovators in their own right. Were it not for Glenn Murcutt, perhaps Australia's most internationally known architect, who thrust the ideals of his mentor into *terra nullius*, one would say the same about Mies van der Rohe! These failures in mentoring seem to me to relate to architects who created a strongly personal formal language, and whatever drove them was best communicated in that form. More open-minded architects like Alvar Aalto, who argued that campuses should always begin baggy to make room for a second and third generation of works by other architects, manifested a generosity that has had a deeper penetration into following generations. People who come to establish platforms of mastery that are springboards for creative innovation tend to choose generous mentors, mentors who open out options rather those who provide security by closing them down.

Research Driven

Mentors are only one part of the story. The architects who make up the Barcelona group Actar are peers who share the same ideas about research-driven architecture. The books that they generate are all researches, never set pieces. Together they work to push the limits of what is understood about the interactions between people and space. Ashton Raggatt McDougall (ARM) is a triumvirate held together by a passion for the authenticity of engagements with the here and now of where they practise, unflinchingly realistic in their approach and loath to cover any discomfort with a slick sheen or considered detail from Prada. They want their research to show. Ushida Findlay conjoined two very different cultures in such a way that a creative space was opened up for both partners – a space that neither could have created alone. In this space research was possible.

As we will see in Zone Three, even those who seem to be loners, like Allan Powell, John Wardle, Sean Godsell and Kerstin Thompson, cluster into like-minded groups for support of a not dissimilar kind. Here, too, lies the role of the critic: people need to have what they are doing recognised for what it is. Only when it has been properly recognised can they move on to the next stage in their innovation. Innovators go to great lengths to find critics or forums that serve this function, this formalising of their achievements. The awards process of the professional bodies can provide a modicum of this kind of recognition, but only a modicum – because of the tendency towards tribal alignments in these processes, such as a refusal to make awards at all when players are from another state or not in thrall to the received values of established masters. I believe that the more effective sounding-boards are those that are set in an international frame, either in their form (international conferences and exhibitions) or in their frames of reference (as when a critic is able to locate works in an argument that is being addressed by creative architects in many different countries).

ARM, National Museum of Canberra, Australia, 2001
This *tour de force* in storytelling completely satisfied the requirements of the client and the board of the museum. Indeed, a didactically rich artefact is a boon to any guide who looks for tags on which to hang a shifting discourse. Canberra is the cockpit of Federal Australia's myth-making, and here lay a problem. While civic narrative expression has been developing strongly in Melbourne, it is held in contempt in other major centres, especially Sydney. Backwash from the international, cool school of modernism that is the dominant position in Sydney – a position complicated by a yachting obsession that tends to technical over-refinement – meant this virtuoso exemplar of its genre was denied a national award by the architectural profession. Later, other onlookers began to dispute the story that was being told through the building, and parts of it became the focus of an argument about Australian history at large. The collage of the plan of the Jewish Museum in Berlin as a floor plan for the Aboriginal gallery, as well as the use of Braille to signal 'Sorry!' on the facade, may have given rise to this debate. In the event, the politics played out on Richard Weller's design for the Garden of Australian Dreams, as it appeared to the lay critics that a garden could readily be changed. Given the agenda of civic architecture, this public debate could be the grounds for arguing for a resounding success for a narrative approach!

Warn and Wetherall, House Glick, Perth 1999, and corrugated iron vernacular, Kellerberrin, Australia
Like many in Perth, one of the most geographically isolated cities anywhere, Geoff Warn can complain of a lack of stimulating discourse. House Glick, however, designed with Jane Wetherall, draws on an environment that is starkly material, leached of any pretension, very much of itself and the use to which it is put. In this it surely learns from informal buildings and fences such as these in the remote town of Kellerberrin. Such pragmatism is also evident in the structures engineers design for the mines – a major focus for innovative design in Western Australia. With a similar ruthless logic, House Glick has a telescoped section. It grows taller to the right to accommodate an artist's workshop and, as it rises, the floor above steps up to form an increasingly intimate series of domestic areas, leaving the living areas with full-height ceilings. A complete roof-deck takes advantage of the night skies.

Raggatt and McDougall of ARM, conceptualise it globally as a centre and periphery problem, feeling that nothing that they do will ever be recognised or acknowledged outside their own tribal area. They fall victim to the fate of the post-colonial, cast off from empire and its metropolitan centrifuge, and doomed to be ignored. They begin to find a virtue in this fate and to exploit it for its creative potential. Others see their own city as uniquely inhospitable to innovation. Geoff Warn in Perth bemoans the intense materiality of the mining state's culture, while gathering commissions for tree-canopy bridge structures that have transformed the urban view of the ecology of rainforests and would be the envy of architects in seemingly more spiritual places. Donovan Hill in Brisbane describe the unique difficulties of working in the most patriarchal state in Australia, and yet out of that self-same crucible they forge an architecture that is changing the way in which we think about site and design in tropical cities. Kathryn Findlay describes the barriers to innovation that she faced in Tokyo, and yet she derives her burgeoning reputation in London from the platform of the work achieved against that resistance.

Donovan Hill, HH House, Brisbane, 1993
During their long march to mastery and beyond, Donovan Hill have confronted a city of patriarchs in which the integrity of each is determined by its separation from all. In their first joint design, they added a frame to the rear of an archetypal bungalow on stilts, an extension that grasps space and connects the house to a wider world. This move was followed by the inscription on the ground of another such 'holding frame', this time one that delineates a civic area of tamed lawn and devotes the periphery of the site to a jungle of tropical growth that joins it perceptually to the Ur-forest that threatens always to engulf the city.

Edge Energy

What they have all mastered is the ability to draw energy from the sense of being on the edge, outside, beyond the pale. This is not simply disenchantment or anomie. It is an energy that would be unavailable if their sense of being outsiders was all that they had. They are all hard at work on a problem area that obsesses them and that has the potential to change the nature of architecture and how we think about it. This resistance is very important. We all know of people who seemed effortlessly able to perform as students, who have excelled in firms. They do establish a mastery but it is one that maintains the status quo: it does not extend the domain. It focuses on technical refinement or hopefully on managing creativity, if that is a possibility. Some people migrate from mastery in architecture to creativity in other realms. Nonda Katsalidis, for example, is an architect whose innovations have increasingly lain in the realm of development packaging. Single-handedly, his vision of high-design apartment building through architect-led funding has transformed the skylines of Melbourne and Sydney. His 92-storey Eureka Tower, now under construction in Melbourne, will be the world's tallest residential tower when completed in 2006, but he feels more on the edge today than he ever has, and not in the mainstreams of architecture or finance. Michael Trudgeon's work has come to exist in the realm of industrial production. It sometimes seems like overscale industrial design. His rethinking of the house leads to the portable kitchen. His work on the ways in which the public can access the collection of the Australian Centre for the Moving Image (ACMI) leads to the design and production of an inhabitable entertainment pod. This work does not sit within any ready-made category for award-giving; it has its antecedents in David Greene's Archigram Cushicle, one of many propositions from that group that sought to extend the range of what architecture can or should concern itself with.

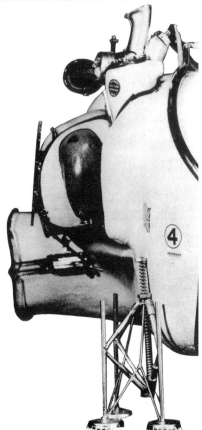

Crowd, HyperHouse exhibition installation in the MCA Seppelt Contemporary Design Awards, Sydney, 1998
Michael Trudgeon of Crowd has made a career in the interstices between architecture and other modes of production, specifically large-scale industrial design. All of the work is on the edge and is not in any way sustained by the usual communities of practice. In this he is part of a new generation of practitioners who define themselves around their research rather than their discipline. Such practice is ever more involved in the periphery of university systems, drawing on the research capabilities of students and rewarding them with involvement in hands-on experience of practical research outcomes. In this, his work realises some of the dreams of Archigram. A recent work, a set of viewing lounges for the Australian Centre for the Moving Image, resembles David Greene's Living Pod (1965). However, the motivation is different from that of the collective that was Archigram. (See case study on Colin Fournier, p 132.) The motivation is less social, more pragmatic. An earlier speculative project by Crowd, conducted in association with Cash Engineering, focused on the future house by incorporating emerging technologies to provide an intelligent, communicative dwelling, one which learnt its climate control from the inhabitant's preferences.

Resistance/Research

Surveying the kinds of innovation that these architects have achieved, I find that they all share another characteristic. In Zone Three I will deal further with the institutional bonds that support mastery and innovation. Here I want to suggest that there has been a fundamental shift in the way in which innovators in architecture see themselves. Previous generations would have defined themselves as 'professionals' first. All around the world (except in Switzerland) architects go into battle to defend this definition of themselves and the institutions associated with being a profession (Switzerland does not have the institutions). There is little explicit discussion about the relevance of the professional model, even when conditions of practice are widely divergent. This is true of both the polarised situation in the USA (which is replicated throughout the professions there, in which there are either huge corporate practices, sometimes with research arms, or very small practices allied to universities) and the less polarised situation in the UK and Australia. I believe that this generation of creative innovators still describe themselves in this way and they support the activities of their institutions, but in fact they operate on a different paradigm. They are researchers rather than professionals. This is very significant. Professions are constructed around exclusive areas of knowledge, which practitioners use to help society. These researchers do not accept the limits to the area of knowledge that standard curriculums define. They research in the medium of architecture. This shift is changing the face of architectural practice all around the world today. For Allan Powell, the research has unearthed his lifelong obsession with the qualities of places and the ways in which only certain levels of abstraction and detail serve to set people in a reverie that re-engages them with their own spatial sensibilities. Kerstin Thompson commenced an investigation into the continuities of surface in her undergraduate thesis, and has developed this through her twisting plane RMIT Technology Estate (RTE) proposal. She brought this to realisation in the Black Swan House at Lake Connewarre, Victoria, in which a tilting arc cuts across the landscape, opening up the contours to sunshine from the north and a view to the south without breaching our sense of the primacy of the land's surface. Other issues of planarity exercise her practice, as with her design for an interstitial brick building at Melbourne's Queen Victoria development. Perhaps Michael Trudgeon has taken the implications of this approach as far as any to date, creating a company, 'Crowd', to hold the shifting alliances of co-researchers that his practice harnesses. Academics who ask difficult questions, students who risk difficult answers, manufacturers and clients who work from proposition towards product – all of these are linked in a system of barter in the pursuit of ground-breaking concepts for living. What all of them demonstrate is that when architecture was made into a profession in the 1830s the wrong body of knowledge was used as the base. Little if any of the research carried out in the medium of architecture is concerned with matters that have progressively become the specialisms of project managers, physicists, engineers and builders. Few, if any, of these are even aware of the imports and effects of spatiality on people, though many of them may be aware through Oliver Sacks[23] of the dramatic difference spatial design makes to the humane management of herds of cattle. Observing architects who are innovators in the emerging generation, it is evident to me that their research-based practice brings linguistic and logico-mathematical intelligence, musical, bodily kinesthetic and spatial intelligence, and naturalist, interpersonal and intrapersonal intelligence to bear on our being in space.[24] If the ensuing practices are to be professionalised – and the ideology of the market makes that a very unlikely venture – then the evidence is that architecture is about our being in space and not about the construction of formal solids. Clearly, then, in establishing the mastery that will become the platform for your creative innovations, you need to choose carefully. Certain choices lead to dead ends, to an honourable but futile attempt to prop up a professional paradigm that consumes rather than provides energy.

Top Kerstin Thompson, RMIT Technology Estate, Bundoora, Australia, 1998

Above Kerstin Thompson, Black Swan House, Lake Connewarre, Australia, 2003
Kerstin Thompson's design (with engineer Peter Felicetti) for a contour-hugging, long-life, loose-fit building for RMIT's northern campus flowed from her investigations into her abiding passion for working with surface contours rather than against them. This emerged as the means to innovation when she did the invitational masters at RMIT. This innovation has been kept in the forefront of her engagement with the landscape of Australia, the oldest and flattest continent.

These forms are not only economical and utile; they also render the slow undulations of the surface plane of the earth evident as a drama that we can re-engage with daily. In the Black Swan House at Lake Connewarre this concept has reached its first full realisation. Thompson is poised for a further innovative breakthrough.

Case Studies
Antwerp

Martine de Maeseneer

The result of conflicts between the larger continental powers, Belgium is the embodiment of a cultural crossroads. Sometimes this has seemed a disadvantage, but today Antwerp is both a portal to a vast networked city, including Brussels and the Ruhr in the golden triangle of Europe, and a self-sustaining force in fashion, furniture and all the personal arts of design with an enviable and ongoing record of innovation in design, production and marketing. Where its neighbours have stolen a march on it – at least in architecture – through a series of government-funded initiatives, these are now out of fashion, and what they supported is in doubt. In Antwerp, however, the innovation is supported by enlightened manufacturers and rides on a tide of entrepreneurial nous that may well have originated in the community of practice of the diamond trade. Certainly this close meshing of informal, trust-based institutions has been replicated in this most recent flowering of European design culture. There are signs that this may be about to extend into architecture. We will know that this is under way when the mastery platform that Martine de Maeseneer has been building over the past decade comes to fruition.

Consider the basis of this platform: in 1997 I wrote of de Maeseneer:[25]

[Ignasi de Sola-Morales's] position on 'weak architecture' is eerily reflected in *Martine de Maeseneer – Ideality • 3 • Lost*. This book arrived courtesy of Yves Nacher and his exhibition 'The Big Shelf, Lost and Found', launched at RMIT on 21 March 1997, an exhibition in which de Maeseneer participated. Nacher's public lecture at RMIT introduced a new generation of (in the main) European architects to Australia. This opening up of new contacts revealed that, no matter how difficult the context, architecture finds ways to emerge – if 'weakly' and 'coarsely'. [This] immediacy … it seems is the 'new' of the emerging generation. The position is gratifyingly expressed in de Maeseneer's book, both in its text, its design and in the work depicted. An increasing awareness of these non-Anglophone developments is very important for us; it helps us to understand that the universalising impact of English language is not necessarily cause of a similar lingua franca in architecture. Reflect on the power of Howard Raggatt's very Australian 'Diatribes'.[26] Like de Maeseneer, but so unlike, language forms design.

There is a coarsely aligned groping towards weakness in current architectures, and it is Ignasi de Sola-Morales who signals the nature of the alignment: 'What is abundantly clear is that, increasingly, metropolitan culture offers us times as diversity … in contrast to the idealist narrative sustained by Giedion … these architectures transform the aesthetic experience … into event' (p 68). Events

Martine de Maeseneer, Logos/Glossy/Glottis office reconversion, Antwerp, 1998 De Maeseneer is very conscious of being 'on the edge' of many social and cultural situations. Growing up with three languages in a country that is an amalgam of two national cultures and in a region that has pioneered the new Europe of the networked super-city of the golden triangle, she is part of the vibrant community of design in Antwerp. The work of her studio is free of many of the formal concerns of her peers to the north. The work finds itself in mirroring and translucency, in interpretations, translations and its slippages. It completes itself in interactions with people, their behaviours and their possessions. Its very fragmentation is a sign of a new approach that her office is testing out in project after project following her first emergence from mastery.

Christchurch

Thom Craig

Thom Craig, transplanted from South Africa to New Zealand, conducted an exhaustive investigation into the frames of translation that had forged his mastery platform: the tropical modernism at the University of Natal, years of practising and then the application of that literacy to a new context. Like several other architects (Nonda Katsalidis in particular) who have chosen to examine the nature of their mastery in practice, the vehicle for expressing his future directions lay in the design of a house for his own family. This 'black box' condensed all of his skills into a single statement. His mastery of 'intimate immensity' is evident in the way in which the building looks almost scaleless from the outside, an effect created by the colouring and by the positioning of windows where they are needed rather than in an externally directed, elevational composition, while inside the uncomplicated white spaces zoom into expansive volume. On this platform Craig has proceeded to build his reputation as one of the most innovative architects in New Zealand, developing, for instance, the design concept for the unusual corrugated flying saucer Westpac Trust Stadium in Wellington, a school in Christchurch and a series of increasingly authoritative houses.

Thom Craig, Close House, Christchurch, 2004
Thom Craig leapt from his mastery platform of considered neo-modernism with the 'black box' that he designed for himself and his family in Christchurch, a city of 300,000 people that had a remarkable record of leadership in modern architecture in New Zealand. The house signalled his departure from the increasingly polite consensus in the city, and asserted a claim to innovative practice beyond the city, demonstrating his share in the authorship of the remarkable Westpac Trust Stadium in Wellington. Since then Craig's practice has been developing through a series of houses that suggest strongly the benefits that will flow when the practice re-engages with the public realm.

Opposite
Thom Craig, Anderson
House, Christchurch, 2002

Right
Thom Craig, Craig House,
Christchurch, 1999

Below
Thom Craig, Le Vailliant
House, Christchurch, 2003

John Wardle, RMIT
Biosciences Building,
Melbourne, 2001
The RMIT Biosciences
Building is the first result of
Wardle's discovery through
the masters of his concern for
a design process that never
turns a corner, that develops
a section that meets the
needs of the programme,
extrudes this and then cuts it
to the length required.

New York

Michael Sorkin

It is often averred that architecture is a nonverbal art, or at least that words do not help, that architects are bad at them and should not be expected to excel in writing. Images are their métier, and if they have a polemic it is in their renderings – like Sir John Soane and his reach for a designed utopia through the delineators Gandy and Basevi – or in their etchings of foreboding dystopias of design, like Piranesi; this despite the evident power of Le Corbusier as a verbal propagandist. It is also a commonplace that the roles of the critic or theoretician and the architect are not compatible. This is an unnecessarily disabling belief, one that deprives architects of a crucial pathway to mastery and a vital tool for transcending mastery plateaus with innovations in design. In a recent critique Nikos Papastergiadis, a keen observer of the creative environments, noted that – in their search for the resistance that can project their work on to a new trajectory – architects are sometimes prepared to engage with all possible mediums except words.

Michael Sorkin is that rare architect who, it seems, has almost deliberately chosen to challenge this perception. His book *Exquisite Corpse*[30] is a delicious account of his critical forays during his time as architecture critic for the *Village Voice*. Over and again he takes no prisoners as he reveals the flawed thinking behind significant projects. It is only when you become aware of the fact that Sorkin is not content merely to be a wordsmith that you realise that he has created numerous hostages to fortune. He clearly reveals the agenda that he as

an architect would have to pursue were he to avoid the pitfalls that he has found so many of his elders and peers stumbling into. Simply to have projected designs into the space that he had created with his critical position would probably have trapped him in gleeful retaliation of a 'those who can do, those who can't critique' nature by those who had been the subject of his clear-headed scrutiny. What could he have done to migrate from a plateau in the mastery of critique (that it was a plateau was signalled by the book's publication – this being a very good way of reflecting upon a mastery achieved) into a quest for a mastery of design? If we look across the moves that characterise the natural history of creative individuals, we might expect him to seek out a group of peers who are in sympathy with his critical position, who are experimenting in the search for their own positions in mastery, and who are unashamed of failures and determined to succeed.

In fact this process had taken place much earlier for Sorkin when he taught at the Architectural Association in the early 1970s, contributing to the intensely political awareness of a group including Katharine Heron, then working on community projects on the Isle of Dogs, Jim Monahan, who was leading an assault on the comprehensive redevelopment proposals for Covent Garden (in which team I was also at work) and Dan Cruickshank, who was occupied with revealing the Georgian history of Brick Lane and many other areas threatened with demolition. This group also enjoyed the precociously intellectual cybernetics

Below and following pages
Michael Sorkin, series of
models, 1994
These images taken in his
New York atelier date from
1994 when Sorkin was first
putting the principles of
Local Code to the test in a
series of innovative designs
for city pieces.

discourse of Ranulph Glanville, and was held together by Grahame Shane's avuncular skills and deep historical knowledge of the process of the city, a process linked to the teachings of Colin Rowe. So it was that when Sorkin began his major push into design, he did not need to re-engage with a group so much as to pick up the threads of this argument, and use it to establish his own position as a designer. He published another book, *Local Code*.[31] This book – on the face of it a theory for the development of cities with genuine differentiations between districts, developing ideas suggested by the later work of Colin Rowe and related to the alternative-futures thinking of urban historian Peter Hall and possibly to NJ Habraken's work on supports – was a defining frame for what he was setting out to explore as a designer. Using the method he proposed in the book, he wrote a code for every design situation that he ventured into, and then set about realising through design what the code implied as being possible. This method established a proposition up front, fully expressed, and then demonstrated through design the ways in which that proposition could be realised with Sorkin as designer.

On reflection, you can see that this work is the counterpoint to his critique of architecture. All too often, he felt, design resembled a lumbering giant, blundering into form independent of programme and in an unarticulated rush of good taste, in the bad sense that fashion can be the latest trend in what is acceptable to the mandarins of what is (wrongly) seen as the single right path of 'architecture'. Sorkin fights for the unique in every site and situation and for the deep intellectual development of a research-based architecture by every designer. These projects engaged teams of enthusiastic supporters from all over the world. They hang in the imaginations of urban architects with just as much force as do the designs of Soane and Piranesi. Producing them, his atelier in New York became a focus of research and innovation in urbanism throughout the 1990s – a period that led to his becoming the focus of radical urban education through his role as professor and director of the urban design programme at the City College of New York (CCNY), a subset of the City University of New York (CUNY) – a position he still holds.

Allen Ginsberg's research shows that ideas take 30 years to move from their expression to their realisation, something that is best exemplified by the analogous history of Ildefonso Cerdà and his plan for extending Barcelona. The socio-economic research and the design of a grid that would meet all conceivable future needs while addressing what ailed the medieval city each took 10 years of work. Another decade was devoted to finding the political means to implementation. Something akin to this is at work in Sorkin's practice. What he designed is becoming possible as a way of making city districts only with the slow coming into being of the communities of practice that will support a nonstandard architecture.

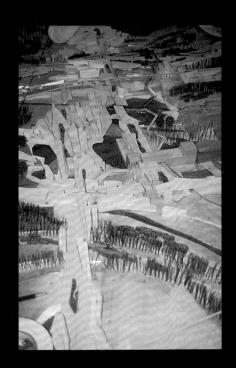

Perth

Geoff Warn

In Perth Geoff Warn used the programme to
reconcile his pessimism about the local building
procurement context with the philosophy of
pragmatism, winning from this a sustainable source
of energy for his inventive endeavours. Educated
under the influence of Archigram cadet Bill Busfield,
Warn was one of a group at Curtin University in
Perth, Western Australia, who early on became
interested in a much wider definition of architecture
than was common anywhere outside the AA at that
time. Their interest in process and in machinery led
to a series of compelling student projects that
haunted the imaginations of generations of students
to come. While Western Australia has a major
mining engineering economic base, no one has
managed to capture that impetus in the creation of
what that early investigation promised. For Warn
the options were stark: move to Europe, where
there were anyway few signs of a take-off in
Archigram-style work, move to the east coast of
Australia or stay and work with what was at hand.
Partly through the continuing optimism of his
mentor, Busfield, who persists in seeing Western
Australia as the California of the future, Warn
stayed. This decision led to the slow development
of a practice, through houses for individual clients
to work in schools and on university campuses. The
persistence of that early curiosity about alternative
forms of practice has paid off in the realisation of a
series of bridges through the canopies of rainforests,
part of a campaign to engage the public in the
conservation of these forests.

Right
Donaldson and Warn,
Goddard Residence,
Fremantle, Australia, 1996/7

Below
Donaldson and Warn,
Tree Top Bridge, Walpole,
Australia, 1997
Geoff Warn has demonstrated
that a mastery developed
through the design of houses
can be extended into
innovative design in the
public realm, be it through a
series of tree-top walkways
over rainforest canopies or in
school and university
buildings.

Singapore

Richard Hassell

Working in the same group of peers as Look Boon Gee, architect Richard Hassell, who joined the programme[34] to examine the mastery that he and his partner Wong Mun Summ had built up over several years of working together, defined the platform on which their increasingly innovative work was based. The partnership commenced with a series of luxury houses, extending to town houses and apartment blocks. In reviewing these works it became apparent that the years the partners had spent working on tropical resorts in Kerry Hill's Singapore practice had given them a mastery in creating lush situations, a mastery that had become almost second nature – so in-built as to be an unremarked quality. The resorts they worked on had no second class: every head that lay on a pillow had to see a stretch of lawn, a fringe of palm trees,

a curve of beach and a breaking wave. Every balcony table had to have a prime view into the forest canopy. This stern school, in which Kerry Hill is an acknowledged leader, had made them into consummate manipulators of the section. Even on the flattest and most constrained of sites they could win for their clients a sense of paradisiacal seclusion. Understanding this, they have managed to incorporate depth into the walls of their high-rise apartment projects – providing an unusual degree of security and dispelling all sense of being on a ledge in the sky. They have won a competition for a metro station with their insistence that it open to the sky and provide users with a feeling of being in a forest. They also designed a monastery complex with a breathtakingly effective ritual circulation system created by the subtle use of the section across a large, hill-top site.

Richard Hassell, Huaguan Avenue House, Singapore, 2001
Richard Hassell and Wong Mun Summ, WOHA Design's journey from mastery to innovation has gone from the creation of 'lush situations' for every visitor in a tropical resort to the design of villas that create oases of tropical delights in the suburbs of Singapore, and on into the innovative translation of these qualities in the public realm through the design of transit stations and a monastery complex.

Photo © Tim Griffith

Mastering Architecture

Richard Hassell and Wong
Mun Summ, WOHA Design's,
Church of St Mary of the
Angels, Singapore, 2003

Left top and middle
Roelof Uytenbogaardt,
University of Cape Town
Sports Centre, Cape Town,
1980

Right
Durbach Block, Dover
Heights House, Sydney,
2004

Bottom left and below
Durbach Block,
Commonwealth Place,
Canberra, 2002
Durbach Block are enchained
to the Cape Town School that
devoted itself to humanising
Le Corbusier's work and
making it relevant to the
needs of a developing country.
Two works by Roelof

Uytenbogaardt resonate with
their major Australian
achievements:
Commonwealth Place,
Canberra, resonates with
Uytenbogaardt's 1970s work
on the Naval Cemetery at
Simonstown while the Dover
Heights House visibly
transcends Uytenbogaardt's
masterpiece, the Sports
Centre at the University of
Cape Town. Commonwealth
Place marks the emergence of
Durbach Block in the public
realm, and their Dover
Heights House points to a
new plateau of innovative
accomplishment.

The Groups in Mastering

Allan Powell, TarraWarra
Museum of Art, Healesville,
Australia, 2004

Afric
lived
in w
view
spa
givi
For
Eng
'do
grea
chi
Cat
jou
chi
eng
for
wit

F
soc

Self-Curating Collectives

Terroir

A new generation of architects is pushing on the doors of mastery and asserting that it has crossed the threshold into creative innovation – making works that change the way we think about what is possible in architecture. French philosopher Hippolyte Taine argued that creative periods are marked by the emergence of a prevailing creative type. Martyn Hook of Iredale Pedersen Hook has suggested that threesomes are leading the way in the new research-led practice in Australia. Others include BKK in Melbourne, Miramar in Sydney and M3 in Brisbane. Without becoming entirely hostage to this idea, the fact is that most of these threesomes do have a member who is embedded in an academy, a member who is embedded in construction and a member who is a spokesperson. Terroir, with Richard Blythe in Launceston, Tasmania, Scott Balmforth in Hobart, Tasmania, and Gerard Reinmuth in Sydney, is just so structured. With Peppermint Bay in Tasmania – a restaurant and bar with a small produce shop – they made their debut in the public realm, their previous work having consisted of houses, alterations and additions.

In this building their mastery is readily apparent. The programme is simply arrayed around a stretched 'Z' line that is the founding diagram of the design, a ramp that emphasises a cut across the site, linking arrival and departure by road and by sea. Three public spaces – a bar, an 80-seat restaurant and a 100-seat function room – fan out towards the view along a fringe of coastal lawn. Each is united with its own external realm: the bar

at the higher contour road end with an external hard-paved area and a view directly back up the estuary; the restaurant with a lawn fringed with trees and glimpses of water beyond; and the function room with the undercroft of a mature oak tree. The 'Z' itself is a wide corridor that channels people effectively into each of these spaces, from the car park on one side, and from the boat pier via the water race and herb wall on the other. It also divides a shop, an industrial kitchen capable of serving 400 or taking on jam production when local fruit is in glut, and the main toilets from the public areas. This is a direct and effective diagram (they acknowledge Stephen Holl's influence here) that is then made manifest in a novel structural solution. This is an advance on Gaudí's hyperbolic roof design of the school of the Sagrada Familia (also tried recently by Greg Burgess at RMIT Bundoora) in which roof purlins, in effect, are supported centrally and arranged in alternating waves at the eaves. This gives a minimal structural thickness and lateral stability almost like a shell. Here the shape of the 'Z' enables the creation of three large, humped shell waves over the public spaces and two crimped, tall waves over the kitchens, housing vents and plant. It is one of those natural, serendipitous solutions that resolve form and function, and that dawn on you rather than being forced on you as evidence of architectural dexterity. The humps over the three public spaces are sliced off and glazed with a pattern of bars, increasing towards the top, which reduces glare inside and from outside resonates with the tree patterns on the hills beyond.

This page and overleaf
Terroir, Peppermint Bay,
south of Hobart, 2004
Terroir is a creative collective, carefully self-curated to include an academic thinker, a pragmatic project realiser and a communicative visionary – though of course, in practice, they all steal each other's clothes! They produce work of increasing vigour, often at first sight ugly, but at a second viewing a new beauty emerges from their ruthless attention to the actualities of their client's needs, the mundane reality of the sites stripped of their symbolic labelling, and their shrewd assessment of local construction capabilities. Their interactions are stimulated by a three-city,

Iredale Pedersen Hook Architects

This young practice is one of a new kind emerging across Australia, a kind that holds lessons for the next generation of architects who aspire to transcend mastery and reach for innovation. Like Terroir, the practice has three partners: one is in a major city and is an academic, one is a rational pragmatist and one is a public voice. The work of these triumvirates seems to develop a level of mastery in a compressed time, perhaps because it is inherently permeable to critique and, in a way, structured around an internalised 'law of small numbers' diversity of approach. The work develops out of a dynamic difference between the partners rather than out of an alignment around the ideas or personality of one member. The structure of the firms is such that they are resilient in the face of indifference. In a sense they provide their own in-built support structures for sustaining innovation, driving each other to further their arguments and supporting the risk-taking inherent in this.

IPH's design for the Reynolds house in Perth exemplifies their approach. This town house for a family who live four hours' drive to the south in Albany, 'a place of large ocean bays where boundaries are defined by the horizon of the sea meeting the sky, (framed by) ever-present granite outcrops', is strung out between an imagining of past 1880s inhabitation and 'the alternative tradition of modernism'. Adrian Iredale, the poet of the three, enchains the work to Hans Scharoun,

Hugo Häring, Alvar Aalto, Günter Behnisch, Bolles + Wilson and Enric Miralles, architects who celebrate 'the particular or specific in lieu of the universal [and] the local and regional in lieu of the international'. The design seeks to complement the landscape and the local tradition. It opens to the horizon, carefully shielding away views of nearby apartments. A 'lean-to roof stretches over the length of the site, eventually leaning back' and cupping the internal space. Signalling Martyn Hook's pragmatism, this 'bull-nose form wraps back above the floor level to provide an external seat and a shelf for electronic equipment'. In conformity with Finn Pedersen's passion for sustainability, 'the north wall allows low winter sun to penetrate deep into the house [and] the mass rear wall collects that sun and shifts and slides to collect cool summer winds. The roof cantilevers in proportion with the height of the glass to eliminate summer insulation. The volume of the room increases [to a high point] where hot air is released via adjustable glass louvres. Recycled jarrah floor joists are split and lapped to form wall panelling, revealing the marks of a previous existence.'

This is an extension to an existing, street-facing house with 'modest introverted spaces, now used as bedrooms. The new bathrooms and wet areas form the transition' between the new and the old. The building in total embodies and expresses the two major themes of Australian house design: a

Iredale Pedersen Hook,
Reynolds House, Perth, 2003

somewhat pessimistic, protective and battened-down, hobbit-like retreat from the vast alien landscape, and an open-air, horizon-embracing manifold that shields you from the extremes of the climate but does not remove you from its immensity. As this house demonstrates, the work of Iredale Pedersen Hook masters its context in three distinct streams of concern. This is evident to them because in forming their partnership they have taken an initial curatorial step. Poetics, pragmatics and systems-thinking are forged together into a dynamic that sharpens the contribution of each partner. This amplification effect is vital to the success of the practice. Iredale's own dwelling is an elaborate play of effects, revealing construction, deconstruction and reconstruction in an almost painterly set of marks. Pedersen's home is a double-volume, north-facing passive solar collector/excluder with a series of internal partitions that seem already on the move to accommodate the changing needs of a young family. And Hook's design for his family home is a strictly existenz-minimum adventure on a tiny site in Melbourne, in which a repetition of elements is manipulated to winnow every available concession from the by-laws. From these ever more defined positions the partners venture into every project separately but then jointly. Each has a plateau of mastery and when these are brought together they create works that are increasingly innovative.

© Robert Frith / Acorn Photo Agency

Opposite and above
Iredale Pedersen Hook,
Reynolds House, Perth, 2003

Fostering Informal Associations

William Lim

Lim was a pioneer of the modern in Singapore, and that means he is not only the co-designer of works like Golden Mile but is also the founder of forums that furthered the business of innovation in architecture, including his various partnerships and Singapore Urban Planning and Research (SPUR). In 1988, however, he founded the Architectural Association Asia, nominally an alumni association of the London school that Boyarsky chaired from 1971 to that date. The articles of association are, however, all to do with replicating for Asian architects some of the benefits perceived to be available to Europe-based members of the AA. The venture began with a difficult convention in Penang in 1988, attended by Peter Cook and Dennis Crompton. The convention was dominated by a series of powerful figures from Asia, and Peter Cook was constrained to voice the view that the work on show was not up to any metropolitan standard. In part, I believe, this was about the difficulties in discerning mastery in territories other than your own. Certainly the effect was to alienate the venture from London as a metropolis, and set it on a determined search for an Asian metropolitan condition that members could set their work within. AA Asia evolved into two distinct activities: a series of lectures given in the Lim apartment by anyone interesting passing through Singapore whom Lim could shanghai for an evening; and a series of study tours for the members to architectural hot spots around the world. In parallel, an ambitious publications programme was launched. The lectures were attended by established and emerging Singapore-based architects and throngs of bright students. Evenings ended in clusters of animated conversation, usually tiered into peer groups but with avid listeners from other generations. Out of this grew an appetite for architectural ambitions in a new generation, ambitions not nurtured in the local school of architecture.

The study tours to Japan, India, Spain, China and Australia confronted members with the work and the discourse of architects from other cultures, and set them reflecting on the nature of their own cultural production. A series of records of these visits, of varying quality, were produced. The process seems to have benefited the middle generation immediately. Architects like Mok Wei Wei have an assurance about the work they are doing and the alliances and differences with international work that has been forged in a conversation between this province and a series of other provinces. A metropolitan level of critique has also occurred through encounters with architects like Ignasi de Sola-Morales and Miguel Fisac in Spain, Fumihiko Maki in Japan, and so on. The horizons of younger members have been further extended and their ambitions broadened. Furthermore, Lim's publications programme has created a forum of discourse in the Chinese-language world that was previously in thrall to a limited set of influences from Philadephia and Chicago.

Lim's genius has been to combine a programme that opened options for his colleagues young and old with a vehicle that has enabled him to extend his own ambitions to hold the ring in a discussion about how to represent the new Asian city, a forum previously dominated by Western scholars. His generosity of spirit overrode racial stereotypes, and he willingly includes Australia and New Zealand in his definition of Asia.

Below left
William Lim, Gallery Hotel, Singapore, 2001

Right and below right
William Lim, Golden Mile, Singapore, 1974
William Lim's career as an architectural innovator spans three plateaus of mastery and subsequent innovation. The first mastery emerged from the Fabian ethic that insists on assessing design in the context of its social consequences – a platform that has become his focus in retirement. Each plateau has been the locus of a significant partnership. The first gave rise to the complex hybrids that characterised the early, nationalist phase of Singapore's development. His

Golden Mile is a rare, built exemplar of a section that has been dreamed of by generations of modernist architects. A tiered wall of apartments with balconies presents a hanging garden to the sun. This sits over car parking, and in the cantilevered area below there is a shopping centre over which there is shaded communal space. In Tampines Community Club and the Church of Our Saviour, Lim worked with Mok Wei Wei to forge a tropical post-modernity of unusual force. Later, with notable artist/architect Tang Guan Bee, he designed his swan-song, the Gallery Hotel, a building that suggests a return to hybridity but this

time with a concern for the culture of its place as well as for the wider metropolitan idea. This was his last major project before he retired to concentrate on teaching and writing about the nature and ethics of new Asian urbanism.

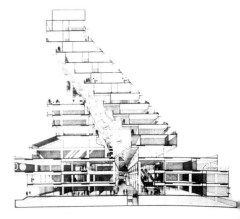

Ken Yeang

For a period in the 1990s Ken Yeang, an AA alumnus with a doctorate in environmental design from Cambridge, ran the Asia Design Forum, as a parallel process that was in a sense a critique of the AA Asia venture. William Lim (with Sonny Chan in Singapore and Ronald Poon in Hong Kong) formed AA Asia as a regional rather than an alumni organisation. The aim of AA Asia was to grow the regional culture from within. It then developed as I have described (see p 118). In the meantime Yeang, determined that his own career as an architect be played out on the international stage in the discursive context of the best possible critiques and not in a circumscribed network (and using the ANY programme as an inspiration),[57] formed the Asia Design Forum. This invited architects from all over the world – but in effect from the East – into a closed session of mutual critique of their most recent work, chaired by me as a moderator and kept on its toes by invited critics, usually from the West.[58] These two-day events ended in a presentation of the discussion by the moderator to invited guests from the professional institute of the city in which the event was held (Sapporo, Kuala Lumpur and Melbourne). An edited transcript of the event was published. Frustrated by the lack of evident outcome from the forum and believing this to arise from the fact that architects were discussing such disparate projects, Yeang changed the format for an event in Taiwan, in which invited architects developed designs for a range of difficult urban situations. These were exhibited and the forum was run in the usual way around these works. These forums developed an increasingly sophisticated conversation and I believe that they had some impact on the mastery of certain young architects. Garry Chang of Hong Kong, for example, began to find his voice in his work in these forums. Frank Ling and Pilar Gonzales Herreiz also established a new reputation through them.

There have been various proposals about systematising the process into a master class along

Ken Yeang, IBM Building, Kuala Lumpur, 1998

Ken Yeang's own architectural ambition arose in the notion of tropicality. An early book, *Tropical Verandah City*, posited a design approach to Singapore that worked with the tropical climate and the lifestyles that it enables. His work fosters an alternative to the explosion of commercial and office complexes that use the curtain wall and air-conditioning technologies that have evolved for very different situations. Yeang's city had few membranes between inside and out, with continuous surfaces that allowed for a relaxed and easy-going interchange between people. He translated this into an alternative vision for the skyscraper office, cut and sliced – as at the IBM offices in Kuala Lumpur – to provide open-air access to every floor, and with a continuous spiral of plant life from the ground to the rooftop pool and entertainment terrace. Later, aware of the difficulty of achieving satisfactory working conditions through natural airflows in high-rise buildings – the cooling breeze tends to disrupt paper-based activity – he turned to groundscrapers. These turn the high-rise on its side and incise a chasm in the ground, drawing the tropical interface deep below the surface.

Le Corbusier, Maxim Gorky, built 1934 and illustrated in Le Corbusier, *Aircraft*, Studio Vista (London), 1935

the lines of the RMIT programme, but the Asian economic meltdown put the venture on hold. It may well commence again, however, in 2005.

Both of these ventures share characteristics that are common to effective support structures in architecture: the convening of cross-generational forums opening up opportunities for enchainment, the discussion of works in unfamiliar contexts, the recording of debate. Both have suffered from some of the problems that all such ventures face, a 'founder's syndrome'[59] that can lead some to reject the forum as being a platform for the personal ambitions of the founder – a kind of overshadowing effect, perhaps, but more likely the inevitable workings of the law of small numbers that suggests that wherever you find unanimity of purpose you are

likely to be approaching a split into two or more schools of thought that gain their energy from their sense of difference. Richard Ho's energetic creation of a forum of Singaporean architects of ambition was invigorating until seemingly it fell apart in a tension between architects who sought to operate within the language of neo-modernism, and Ho's own growing sense – as I see it – that he needed to connect more overtly with the specifics of the culture and poetics of Singapore as it has developed since his childhood in shop-houses and in the east coast villa of his grandfather. Some of these architects, who were very close, no longer communicate despite Lim's attempts to argue for architecture as a house with many rooms.

Ken Yeang, Guthrie Pavilion, Kuala Lumpur, 2000
The design for the Guthrie Pavilion, a form of country club, eschews the usual 'Tudorbethan' decoration of the type in Malaysia, insisting on a form that is forward-looking with wide, oversailing shade wings, even if in his enthusiasm for the future he draws on an iconography of the modern first identified by Le Corbusier in his book on aeroplanes – see the Maxim Gorky (p 122).[60]

Partnerships for Life and Practice

Julian Feary and Katharine Heron – Enchaining Art

Katharine Heron studied architecture at the Architectural Association School of Architecture in London, graduating in 1970. She comes from a creative family. Her grandparents were enlightened manufacturers who commissioned leading designers, supported the garden-city movement and were involved in individual acts of creativity including poetry. Her father, Patrick Heron, was the famous painter and critic who chose to establish his studio at St Ives in Cornwall. Her childhood was centred on 'Eagle's Nest' – a house at Zennor in Cornwall surrounded by a garden of rooms created to fend off the wind and capture the sun of all seasons. The shrubs that provide this shelter are hardy, wind-resistant plants from New Zealand. It is difficult to imagine a place more redolent with architectural impulses; the huge granite boulders of the hill-top frame the house and the garden in an elemental set of compositions that inspired Katharine's father into investigations into the 'shape of colour'. The penetration of shafts of light into space and a keen awareness of the vivid palette of natural materials were in turn the key for her fascination with architecture. Her parents continued the Fabian activism of her grandparents, and her attraction to architecture combined her spatial interests to a lively understanding of the essential entwinement of politics and the built environment.

Her early career[61] involved the delicate business of designing and building the gallery at Stoneypath, Dunsyre, in Scotland, for Ian Hamilton Finlay. It also involved a number of alterations and additions to existing houses, designs that were suffused with her sense of light and vivid colour. This early partnership designed uniquely entwined apartments in a terrace on London's Isle of Dogs, arranged to provide all four with a view of St Paul's Cathedral to the west (now obscured by Canary Wharf) and the Thames to the east. Living in one of these, she became strongly involved in the needs of local children and worked to establish the pioneering urban farm at the Mudchute. At this time she taught at the AA in the first-year unit of Grahame Shane, working with a team including cybernetician Ranulph Glanville, Covent Garden activist Jim Monahan, critic Michael Sorkin and me as a theorist. At the AA she became friendly with Robin Evans and in due course he and his family moved into one of the Isle of Dogs apartments, which were a staging post for a number of people who have had a significant role to play in the educational life of these times. Her interest in architecture as a support for creative ventures grew through her work on the Pier Arts Centre, Orkney, in which she pioneered a briefing approach that led to a deep understanding of the assemblage of necessary components that such centres require if they are to thrive.

Julian Feary grew up in Auckland, New Zealand. He studied architecture at the University of Auckland and in the final year of his first degree he and the leading lights of his year organised a student conference that was famous for its self help-ecological ethos. An abandoned brickworks was the site for the conference. Delegates had to build their own shelters and camp out on the site.

Right
Feary Heron, Cabinets at Manchester Road, London, 1976

Below left and right
Feary Heron, Big Painting Sculpture, London, 1996–8
Feary Heron's design combines Katherine Heron's vivid sense of colour and its relationship to form (seen on the right in a kitchen design from the 1970s) and Julian Feary's concerns for the responsible making of the built environment. Their Camden House forges a studious environment tailored to the needs of a scholarly couple. The windscreen for Stag Place off Victoria Street in London is a wonderful realisation in three dimensions of Patrick Heron's lifelong concern with the shape of colour. The work took intense research into materials, structure and lighting. The enamel panels capture the dynamic between form and hue in a range of colours. Neon has been found that matches these hues, lighting the edges of the panels at night. This is a practice that has mastered collaboration as a route to innovation both in design and in organisational stewardship.

Vorberg and Kirchhofer – VK Architecture

'A thousand years of democracy and what do you have? The cuckoo clock!', or words to that effect, sneers Orson Welles as the villain in *The Third Man*. Despite or perhaps because of its unique cantonal federation, Switzerland has an enviable history of innovation in architecture since modernism. Some would say that its pre-industrial vernaculars are so charged through the extremes of terrain and climate that they are uniquely nuanced to every valley system, and that they embed ritual behaviours that have evolved from various communal survival strategies. This could be a profoundly conservative heritage, one enforcing the extensions of the traditional into the kitsch that have often bedevilled Austria and Germany. However, aside from certain excesses of geraniums, Swiss architecture has drawn from its history a propensity to rethink the needs of every valley in unabashedly contemporary terms. Our fathers' libraries were stocked with books on Switzerland's modern villas of the 1920s. A journal ingloriously entitled *AC* (Asbestos Cement) disseminated work after work of cost-effective, Occam's Razor-obedient works from Brazil to Timbuktu. Le Corbusier is really a Swiss thinker who – in some lights – has succumbed to inappropriate internationalist ambitions. Zurich is graced by one of his last and lightest works. Generations later Peter Zumthor is able to draw from the traditions of timber construction and the exigencies of avalanche-prone hillsides, the shingle chapel of St Benedict in Somvix. Later, he thinks his way from that invention to the glass shingles and concrete core of the Bregenz Museum of Art.

Yet it is not useful to speak of 'Swiss architecture' except in a propagandist manner. Any examination of what has been achieved dissolves into the specifics of each region. Take the Ticino. Although it has only recently achieved its own school of architecture under the aegis of Mario Botta, but led initially by Aurelio Galfetti, this canton has a distinctive and uncompromising modern tradition through the pioneering works of three generations of architects. These architects have been able to extract the historic elemental characteristics of their region, such as the steep-sided valleys, ancient stone fortifications, the massive and singular materiality of the buildings, the stone walls and roofs, and concoct from this an idiom that is uncompromisingly of the present and yet profoundly respectful of the past. The initiating moment for this in the 1960s lay in the works of Rino Tami, Alberto Camenzind and Tito Carloni, whom Vorberg and Kirchhofer cite as the 'grandfathers' of the Ticino enchainment. The 'great-grandfather' was Giuseppe Terragni, whose Casa del Fascio in Como, just across the border, continues to cast a liminal shadow over the entire region. The teachings of Aldo Rossi, especially his treatise *L'architettura della città* influenced the next generation: Luigi Snozzi, Aurelio Galfetti, Mario Botta, Livio Vacchini, Flora Ruchati, Bruno Reichlin, Fabio Reinhart – the 'fathers'. In the 1980s, the 'descendants' drew on Rossi's work on the exemplars of ancient architecture and created a rash of tower and bridge houses across this southern region as Botta and others saw their

Right
The design of Soabbia resonates with the church gable on a hill above

Below left and right
VK Architects, Housing, studio and gallery complex, Soabbia, Switzerland, 2000–ongoing
Vorberg and Kirchhofer chose to relocate their practice in an area of Switzerland that both appeals to their core sensibilities and situates them on the edge of their natural support systems. A slow but wide practice with many facets of mastery and innovation has been their reward. A tower near Zurich railway station was an early inspiration for their desire to combine planting and building. A simple facade in the Ticino inspired their shift to the south with the design of the housing complex at Aurigeno. Here they found sustenance in the pioneering work of architects like Snozzi, who radically reinterpreted the vernacular in an uncompromisingly rational manner. Their latest complex, in Soabbia, is a softer and freer interpretation of how to live, work and garden in this region.

chance. Some would argue that Botta has taken this into a romanticism that is cloying, and argue that innovation has shifted to a focus on Basle. The austerity of Snozzi's vision, and the way in which it reveals the ancient and sets these remnants back into the action of the modern networked city that Galfetti's infrastructure designs have done so much to bring into being, is still widely respected, however.

Vorberg and Kirchhofer are two architects from Zurich families who met while working in an office after studying – six years apart – at the Eidgenössische Technische Hochschule Zurich (ETH), then still under the influence of Aldo Rossi. Rossi in this period was known as a Rationalist, and his Rationalism aligned comfortably with the older tradition of Gottfried Semper, whose design for the ETH is one of the most clearly ordered hierarchical designs in all Europe. The ETH is an edifice so clear in its circulation and structural logic that to walk through it is almost to have your mind combed. Semper's theories about the evolution of architecture were the first to challenge the singular origin in the primitive hut and to place alongside this ontology an alternative derived from weaving and the tent. Rossi planted firmly the notion that the architect must imagine a future for the city that may be completed only centuries after it has been conceived, and his signature achievement of the period was La Gallaratese, a housing block on the edge of Milan that contained within its form redundant spaces that only future generations were expected to utilise. Both of these

theorists have imbued the Swiss architectural domain with an independence of thinking and a sense of social responsibility that has survived the post-modern relativism that has sapped the energy of discourse elsewhere.

Kirchhofer had a childhood in Africa and hankered for warmer climes and Vorberg is from Protestant Zurich. With vastly differing backgrounds, they shared an attraction for the south. As Kirchhofer wrote during a series of email exchanges with me: 'The culture of Italy has always fascinated both of us – the medieval town layouts, the contrasting renaissance grandeur. Our year-long trip through the Americas – the rigid Spanish town layouts and the playful use of courtyards – these reinforced our architectural perception.' Together she and Vorberg were attracted to the Ticino in Switzerland and eventually moved there, removing themselves from the support of their peers in the north and throwing themselves into the very different loyalties of the Italian-speaking south. In the north they had won two cantonal competitions and hoped this would continue in the south. This has proved to be a vain hope. Local competitions are more local than the ideal would suggest they should be. Nevertheless they commenced their southern practice with a remarkable housing complex – Aurigeno – that sits clearly between the ideals of early Rossi and the more extreme positions taken by Botta and Snozzi. 'What drew us to the Ticino, besides other considerations, was the stark vernacular architecture which we wanted to interpret into a modern language. This we tried to

do, and (on reflection) it's not surprising that all our clients came from north of the Alps.' They had a similar romantic notion of the value of the indigenous. 'The local Ticinese did not appreciate our buildings at all, too much did it remind them of their not so distant poverty.' Vorberg and Kirchhofer commenced work on the construction of their own mini-utopia – Soabbia – a courtyard of dwellings, work studios and art gallery. This is radical building drawing on first principles for energy-efficient construction, sheathing a blockwork structure in deep insulation protected from the elements in corrugated aluminium, and yet the facades make long cast references to an Italianate church on the hills above. In some ways, this complex looks out and connects to the pre-existing fabric of Bellinzona. In others, it creates a Zurich courtyard in which a northern urbanism is entrenched. Yet in other ways, it is resolutely fixed on the southern horizon and the edge of the tectonic plate of Africa. They see it as 'a miscellany of ideas. The buildings, arranged around a central court, stem from courtyards seen in Lombardy, the University of Pavia and Spanish colonial buildings. The exposed concrete and concrete blocks are surely the heritage of Snozzi and Botta, and the corrugated aluminium must have its roots in colonial Africa!'

What their practice reveals is a nuanced positioning between a common intellectual heritage articulated by Rossi (before he abandoned his social ideals and adopted a market-driven post-modernist style) and particularities of the Ticino. In the Ticino, and not of it, they have positioned themselves midway between the poles of Snozzi and Botta, and have attracted the support of neither camp. Perhaps it is only the lack of understanding for the way in which domains split into fields that has deprived them of the allies their position deserves. They have another take on this: 'So it is actually quite clear – even though we have been warmly tolerated since arriving here, two "zucchini" full of wonderful ideas – that we can't belong in any camp in the Ticino architectural scene – that we are hybrids on a foreign soil. Despite this lack of a common social background with Ticinese architects, we find the situation most congenial to our way of working. In fact, not belonging to any school, party or clan allows us the freedom to play by our own rules. As Dostoevsky puts it: "To go wrong in one's own way is better than to go right in someone else's".' This last quotation is uncannily similar to Robert Kegan's definition of mastery,[63] what I have called innovation – the invention of your own way, the moment at which the pattern resides within, and yet at which paradoxically you are able to view your practice from outside. Vorberg and Kirchhofer go on to define that way, and in so doing link themselves to the new, research-based practice mode that characterises innovative architects today: 'Architecture is a small part of our daily agenda these days. We are caretakers, renovators, gardeners, financial jugglers and so on. It's become a very diverse world. I remember looking over a mentor's shoulder in the early 1970s as he wrote in his notebook: "The generalist is dead". Maybe today he would think differently.'

Migrating Contexts

Colin Fournier

Of course, I could consider Colin Fournier's trajectory to mastery and beyond in the context of the natural history of the creative individual. There are stunning alignments between his personal history and the accepted conditions for becoming a creative innovator. He was born the illegitimate child of a distinguished French physicist, who elected to leave France to continue the fight against fascism, and a distinguished British academic. Colin was brought up in a peripheral environment that was very much focused on ideals and excellence. In his personal style he projects an aura of otherworldliness. Seeming ultra-English to the French and yet assumed to live in Paris when in England, he has the manner and talent of a continental intellectual. In his personal life he has continued the transcendence of his upbringing. Married to a distinguished Austrian artist, the partner and child of his first marriage located first in Los Angeles and then in New York – could there be anyone more interstitial to the command centres of Western culture? Rumoured to be colour-blind, numerate in a domain in which visualisation is a dominant attribute, he made his way into architecture as if into an extreme form of physics in which the unknowns and variables defied comprehension and demanded his attention for that reason. His early work on modelling urban situations could, he was very aware – citing parallel happenings in the USA – have the unintended consequence of creating tools that would be of use to the developers whose crass operations he sought to render transparent to the community. In this one

sees an enchainment to the ideals of his physicist father, who refused to work on nuclear armaments. In his career he has returned many times to the challenge of understanding the algorithms of urban development, and this has led him into unlikely situations as an expert consultant to major corporations in delicate Middle Eastern terrains. And yet it is his adept seeking out of allies that I wish to concentrate on in this partial study.

Architecture is the domain whose complexity attracted him and he studied at the Architectural Association and not, as one might have expected, at the London School of Economics. At the AA he was early drawn into friendship with Bernard Tschumi – partly on a Francophone sympathy. Both of them had sought out the centre of experimental architecture in Europe in the 1960s – the Archigram group. Together they became tutors in the Diploma School taught by Peter Cook and as is acknowledged in the Archigram Exhibition (London 2004), Colin became a leading player in the Peter Cook-led design for the Monte Carlo Casino. Very early in his career Colin had the job of giving form to an Archigram idea and developing an exegesis for Archigram, and – together with Tschumi on this occasion – negotiating the design towards realisation. Sadly, this proto-ecologically responsible, buried building was not realised as the client fell victim to the 1970s fuel crisis. It was on the tide of this crisis that Colin became involved with a major international consulting company in a series of urban initiatives in the Middle East from a base in Los Angeles. His first wife, Christine, was at

Right
Colin Fournier with Ron Herron and Ken Allinson, Monte Carlo 'Palm Tree' scheme, Monte Carlo, France, 1971

Below and overleaf
Colin Fournier and Peter Cook, Kunsthaus, Graz, Austria, 2003
Like many 'second' cities, Barcelona and Melbourne chief amongst them, Graz differentiates itself from Austria's first city through a radical architecture of innovation. Here this draws closely on a distinct local literary tradition, and it insists on interpreting the metropolitan ideas through the lived experience of its province and not through

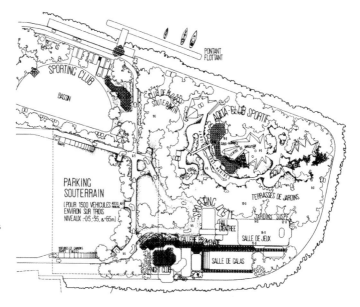

borrowed forms. A recognisable genre of sharply pointed buildings has emerged, fractured and faceted like Bruno Taut's dream of a glass architecture, and owing much to an interpretation of local geography. When the citizens of Graz agreed to an international competition for a new arts complex, they called for a work that would further distinguish their city. Because the local culture is so strong, there was every likelihood

the same time developing her practice in international law and their careers seemed in many ways on parallel tracks towards an increasingly globally integrated world. Here, in his middle career, a curtain is drawn across a plateau of mastery as an international urban consultant. He emerges from this period with his early attributes still in place. His alliances are all intact, and his second marriage drives his interests back from a corporate managerial trajectory towards concrete artistic accomplishments.

He re-engaged with Peter Cook, who had become professor of architecture at the Bartlett School of Architecture in London, a position he used to wrest from the Architectural Association the reputation for being the home of experimental architecture in Europe. Colin became a professor of urbanism at the Bartlett. Together he and Peter Cook entered a competition for a Museum of Art in Graz, Austria, and the dynamics of Monte Carlo reignited in their partnership. Colin led this winning design through design development to realisation, and achieved for himself and his early mentor a crucial epiphany – the demonstrated transcendence of a plateau of theoretical mastery by a building that is both supremely at home as an urban object and that realises many of the liberating dreams of

Archigram's fundamentally democratising aim of making architecture relevant to everyone, be they children, shop assistants, tradespersons, art lovers, layabouts or industrialists. Colin's favourite account of this remarkable building – the friendly alien – is a series of drawings by schoolchildren that gently anthropomorphise its form or re-create it as a whale, or a cow with distended udders, or as a glove …

The building is all of a piece with the early urban modelling ideals that sought to put the development of the city in the hands of its citizens, and it captures people's imaginations by making them realise that, after all, anything is possible and that it can be accessibly fun.

Of course, this took place in very specific circumstances. Colin chose his field in the domain of architecture very early on, understanding that Archigram is considerably more radical than it appears on the face of things to be. In this his English heritage shows, because the basic propositions of Archigram are not surfaced in neo-Marxist dialectics, as would have been respectable on the continent. The deeply unsettling challenges to elitist architectural cultures, be they neo-classical, neo-modernist or structuralist, emerge by stealth. Well, not stealth as strategy – that would be that a local design would win – very unlike the situation in Bilbao. This was a competition run from a position of strength, and this enabled the city to embrace Cook and Fournier's design without any sense of loss. They were adding to an already vibrant culture of architectural innovation. The 'friendly alien' has provoked many responses, almost all affectionate. Amazingly, it seems very much at home in the red-tiled city.

too obviously planned, and would be spotted and exposed by many island ironists. Cedric Price is often considered a thinker on a similar track, but his jujitsu proposals – profoundly influential as they have been – did not partake of the rebellious sensuality that characterises Archigram's best works, be they Ron Herron's Walking City in New York (1964), Mike Webb's Sin Centre (1959–62) and his Cushicle (1966–7), David Greene's Living Pod (1965) or Peter Cook's Adhox (1971). These are all 'lush situations' that bring into everyday play the joys that past centuries had reserved for small elites.[64] This is the one architectural movement, of all those since the 1930s case study houses, that has brought the possibility of a continuum of spatial experience into our grasp. The friendly alien is 'souvenirable',[65] and one can imagine it on the mantel shelves of homes, symbolising the possessors' acknowledgement that they have had their spatial intelligence reawakened through child-like joys. This is in contrast to the ways in which the sterner outcomes of architectural theories of the 'existenz minimum' or 'luxury trade maximums' kind have done nothing but alienate the popular imaginary, driving architecture as a practice on to the fringes of experience, with only 3 per cent of the population able to 'afford' a purpose-designed home.

It is important to realise that these positionings are not accidents – although the timing of them is entirely subject to chance. Colin is not trying to occupy every field in architecture's domain; he chooses very specific fields of discourse, enchainment and peer support, and even when it is difficult for others to see the thread, it is there underlying every step in his trajectory. An interviewer[66] once asked Iannis Xenakis whether he acknowledged that his works were all about the same enquiry. He replied in the affirmative. 'Have you ever tried to be different?' the interviewer continued. 'Well,' said Xenakis, 'when I was young I did try, but I soon discovered I was the prisoner of myself.' This kind of 'imprisonment' is common to innovators. It is the self that is curated from mastery to creativity, over and again, plateau by plateau, leap by leap.

Louis Kruger

Is innovation international? This is the obverse to the question about mastery, to which the answer that I have given is a resounding 'no!' This 'no' is not, however, an endorsement of internationalism. Internationalism asserts a single context in architecture, as much as it does in any other field, for example, accountancy. That context, I have argued, is singular only in that innovations that transform a domain are recognised in metropolitan (lower-case 'm') discourse, and can be asserted only in the provincial actualities in which they are forged, be they architecture or … accountancy. Architects are prone to despise accountants and 'creative accounting' is not an epithet anyone aspires to. Yet these are both internationally pervasive practices, and practitioners can move freely enough around the world in the pursuit of them. Accountancy has a representation in everyday life that is enviable to architects and this has much to do with its historic and international consistency. However, the most thoughtful of accountants[67] know that 'standards' of ethical behaviour are inevitably played out in provincial actualities, and that they reach only fitfully towards a more general, metropolitan consciousness. For these more thoughtful people, there is a continuing wonder in the many tensions between these two poles, an increasing awareness that transactions across cultures need to celebrate these nuances consciously, not to obliterate them in fits of self-righteous indignation – an emotion that is a remnant of the old imperial certainties that so readily defined centre and periphery.[68] Accountancy

goes back to the cuneiform origins of writing, and when it is conscious of that history it is aware of its many houses and their many rooms – even as it insists upon certain principles in practice, and even if these are inevitably interpreted in different ways in London, New York, Houston, Kuala Lumpur and so on. Keeping honest is achieved by insisting not on a London standard, but on interpolating between the standards of every place, and constantly translating back and forth between places towards a common, metropolitan understanding. This is the actuality of the post-colonial world, but imperialist attitudes die hard. London, New York and Tokyo are acknowledged command centres in the dissemination of information and a cascading hierarchy still descends from these poles – with much disputing about who merits inclusion in the second and third tiers. Yet as Celeste Olalquiaga has delightfully shown, the counterflows – from places that are not even ranked in this neo-imperialist conversation – are where the real interest lies, where innovation is to be found.[69] Those who attempt to control the flow of information by being the arbiters of the new, watch these counterflows closely! It is to our growing awareness of these flows that the role of lower-case 'm' metropolitan discourse owes its current developments.

Perhaps in architecture this active-listening pluralism translates into an endorsement of the continuing nexus between the provincial and the metropolitan in creative work. This very rarely happens today. Architects embrace either their

Right and below
Louis Kruger, Casa Bellomo,
Adelfia, Italy, 2004
In this complex of four
houses, three attached and
one freestanding, Kruger uses
the local store of geometric
forms to meet client
expectations of the formed
public face of the house. Half
hidden below is the basement
with openings to a sunken
garden: this is the level the
family occupy all year round,
returning upstairs to the piano
nobile only for the most
formal of occasions.

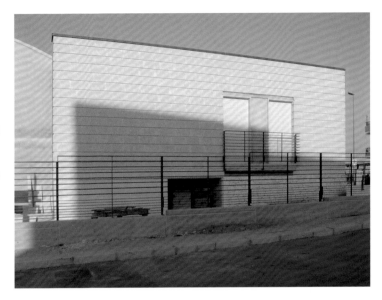

province or an imagined Metropolis. Every country is dominated by Metropolitan architectural certainties that blind it to much of the work that is done in its own provinces. Italy, for example, is said to be dominated by two blind schools – one in Venice, one in Rome – blind because they see only that which they choose to call 'architecture' – a singularity that they themselves have defined. Their international vision is wide, and draws in work that they admire from all around the world. Yet their ability to 'see' locally is far less developed, to the cost of the continuum between architecture and the general public. From these centres scholar-architects fly out to the provinces on a Tuesday morning to preach, and to their citadels they return on a Thursday evening.

In the far south there is a new school of architecture in Bari. It has recently graduated its first cohort. Situated within the provinces but concerned not to be of them, at Bari they preach a historical, regionally inflected, orientalist internationalism through Roman lenses, though they network assiduously abroad and claim to be the foremost school of the eastern Mediterranean. In small towns around this school, but below the horizon of Rome or Venice – and indeed of Bari, even though many locals teach there – they see only an architectural desert. Yet in these towns practitioners have built up a body of work that would shine brightly on the agenda of architectural innovation, certainly in terms of the provision of architecture as a service in every community. The story of Louis Kruger is exemplary. His story

emerges because, as a migrant, he has a network that connects him directly to London and on into the world. Because he is a migrant, he is not inwardly subservient to the geopolitical Metropolis that the Italian power system continues to operate. Working with a clientele of the *petite bourgeoisie* to begin with, and through that attracting the attention of the builders themselves, he has progressively worked to understand the southern house and develop an architecture that addresses its values and behaviours. With the builders he has completed a series of apartment buildings that transcend the particular angst of negotiating between observations of what people actually do and what they believe that they do. Kruger is the son of an architect who was a Witwatersrand-trained modernist from one of the leading schools of modernism in South Africa, a country viscerally tied to Europe and America in defiance of its British hegemony, and whose practice began with a house for an accountant. This school (which my father also attended – with Robert and Denise, née Lakofsky, Scott Brown) regionalised modernism through amalgamating Breuer, Schindler, Mies and Neutra. It was at first closely connected to Le Corbusier, and Neutra visited late in his life. It was, however, in Oscar Niemeyer's mediated New World modernism that it found the closest parallels to an achievable architecture.

Louis Kruger married a migrant from Bari and they returned to that area to raise a family. In ways that are now familiar to us, Kruger fits the mould of the creative innovator. An outsider, growing up on the fringes of a powerful ideal, shifting always into

situations of danger but of personal growth, he arrived in 1983 and began practising near Bari, listening to his clients and observing how they behave. Sure, they demand a piano nobile, but it is always to sit upon a half-submerged basement, which they insist upon, but which they also insist is of little consequence. All the talk is of the reception room level and all the imagining is of the designer furniture with which this space will be kitted out. Bedrooms are above, always. Roof terraces are a must – for the hot season, it is said, but in practice for a possible future extension. A certain formality and a certain materiality must be projected. And yet, when the move into the new home is finally made, all of the old furniture is put into the basement. So is a stove, so are deep freezers. So is a television. When he visits on post-occupancy issues, the piano nobile is deserted. The basement has been upgraded with a fireplace – a 'hearth' – and dark-stained, wooden beams. Observing this, Kruger added a bathroom to the basements in his designs and a sunken garden next to it. And he upgraded the specification to make a second kitchen. Word spread: 'Here is an architect who knows how to make a good basement!' But it is a delicate business. The architect can push the envelope only so far. The piano nobile must be seen to be the focus, even if it is only for entertaining strangers or for special events. As he discovers where the tensions are, and how they can be resolved, his architecture gets quieter, more materially bedded down. His competitors – engineers, often as not – make suburban-scale,

sub-Calatravan roofs in order to compete. Kruger is not alone in his quest for a local architecture that respects his father's internationalist ideals – ideals, after all, of extending the best of spatial organisation to the multitudes through the operation of the principle of parsimony.

Why is it then that Rome and Venice ignore the efforts of these architects who are embedded in towns that lie beyond their intellectual horizons? True, Milan has exported an exhibition of works in small municipalities all around Lombardy, and this quietly effective work shows how powerfully locally embedded practices can improve places that more overtly formal work by 'star' architects or designers can only internationalise. Where do such locally active practitioners turn for the critical attention that could recognise and foster their development? Currently they rely on their own confidence in the importance of their role in the often difficult continuum between their own spatial intelligence, their own proposition about architecture and the often unconscious preferences of the people whom they serve. Kruger, for example, finds that his negotiations with particular owners can unravel when they fail to distinguish between symbol and actual. This creates an angst that can become an internalised doubt rather than a tool for sharpening the proposition. Fortunately circumstance has provided Kruger with a network to call upon when the doubt is extreme. Surely it should be the role of the academies to promote such discourse in every province?

Establishing Poles

Sean Godsell

In a recent book on Sean Godsell,[70] I note that moment when English rugby player Jonny Wilkinson pauses before taking a kick and, looking wistfully sideways, raises his hands to waist height and brings them together as if slowly squeezing the space between them. Asked why he did this, he replied that through this gesture he was able to remove the crowd and render himself completely alone on the field with the task at hand. This anecdote, recounted to Godsell, brought an immediate flash of recognition. Few other architects of his generation bring to practice the total concentration of the athlete. Few other architects today practise in a way that is so unmediated between themselves and the production processes of architecture. That is not to say that Godsell is a lonely genius – he has a talent for attracting the loyal enthusiasm of his associate Hayley Franklin, of the flow of students through his office, and he has in his life partner a design journalist who is both strong supporter and worthy adversary. Yet where others have embraced all of the collaborative tools of digital design, Godsell and his team produce every drawing in pencil on trace. The ideas are pressed out through the mark of the hand. There is also no mediation between Godsell and the construction process. He will intervene directly and physically to remove work in progress on a site that is leading to an eventual compromise between what has been visualised and what has been built. The consequence of this lack of mediation is a body of work that – since he clarified his ambitions during the design of his own house in Kew, Melbourne (in the framework of the RMIT masters) – has a controlled intentionality that is extremely rare. Like most architects whose work endures as an influence on future generations,[71] Godsell deals with a small set of ideas but the rewards are growing. The Kew House, the Carter Tucker House and the Peninsula House are a journey into an increasingly timeless perfection in the combining of space and construction, one that Godsell sees as of the Kyoto spirit. His institutional works translate these concerns into the public realm with an increasing assurance. There is also a constant strand of self-funded experiments that seek out the ways in which this architectural quest can provide support to those in need. They go beyond the usual provisions of a client–architect relationship – he has designed and manufactured emergency housing from park benches to containers that can be dropped into disaster zones. The ideas are simple, like including in every plan since his earliest house in Faraday Street a journey from the street to the back of the site, giving glimpses of spaces before any of the rooms of the house are entered. Simple ideas, but related to profound notions of how to encompass a world in a tiny shell, so that the journey into the house is a journey from the troubles and distractions of the world towards a sanctuary of repose and contemplation. The construction of the houses is more and more about the same journey. In the Peninsula House, a glass roof floats below a lath screen. The effect is that of being sheltered by a leafy tree. Details in this architecture are not there to impress you with their virtuosity; they are there

Sean Godsell, Peninsula House, Mornington Peninsula, Victoria, Australia, 2002

The Peninsula House is the most perfected of Godsell's houses to date. The approach is deceptive, a low carport on the crest of a remnant dune shields that the house from view. A pathway leads down one side of the house, stepping down the dune to a lower level between slender columns and an oversailing roof of glass and lath. As you reach the public, double-volume areas of the house, your host can offer the choice of two external spaces and the living room that interconnect with variable degrees of fluidity, depending on the occasion. Or you may be invited into the study that is tucked in back against the dune, a retreat with fireplace and comfortable sofas. Access to the private areas of the house, including a bathroom that opens on to a courtyard through a tilting glazed wall, is through a secret panel in the side wall of the living space. This is a house in which the rituals of the client's public and private behaviours have become ligaments of the spatial arrangement and the construction. Screens rise and fall, openings are revealed, all according to the nuances of every imagined social and personal situation. Above all, this is a house in which you are in the universe, not bunkered away from it. It is supremely optimistic about being.

to lift the burdens of gravity, and put you in touch with yourself and the universe. This architecture squeezes the noise out of your life and puts you in the position of being timelessly in touch with yourself or with your family, your friends or your colleagues. This comes about because of the intense concentration of Godsell's process, the overarching ambition to achieve a spiritual lightness, in a grounded place, with the thinking etched into paper and re-etched into construct. This is a polarising process in the community of practice. Few of his colleagues approach this kind of concern, an arcing from concept to minute detail and back. And there is an athlete's hyperbole in some of Godsell's public utterances that threatens those not so committed.

Allan Powell, TarraWarra Museum of Art, Healesville, Australia, 2004
The entry forecourt to the TarraWarra Museum of Art is a holding frame for the weather. Shadows move across the floor and up on to the containing walls. There is little here that traditionalists can grasp. The building eludes classification, dissolves any rationalist hierarchy of structure and skin. Powell continues to push into zones of experience that operate in a dream-like sate. This is innovation without cleverness, and it baffles many of his colleagues, to his delight and consternation.

again. If anyone has come close to describing his architectural ambitions it is the late Ignasi de Sola-Morales in his discussion of 'weak architecture',[73] but Powell's work exemplifies this approach far better than the architecture cited by Morales. Powell quotes with great pride the frustration of a supportive builder who burst out with: 'There are no details in your buildings! Everything is floating! And yet somehow something very forceful results!'

Are there followers? Certainly there are architects who have been taught by Powell and who use some of his stratagems. Stephen Jolson has taken Powell's dictum about 'stepping on to a platform on which elements are arranged' to heart and tried this to various effects in a series of large coastal houses. What has yet to emerge is a group inspired by the problem itself, though internationally there are peers whose interests are similar.

Powell seeks a metropolitan validation for his work through his active seeking out of a critique that is connected to an international perspective. Melbourne has a strong scholarly focus on its own architectural history and Powell and could have aligned himself with this alone. However, he has involved himself in the international process of the RMIT programme and an ongoing critical dialogue with me. This architect has created an enchainment structure that supports his particular sense of breakthrough across his domain. The popular success of the Di Stasio House and the popularly recognised primal rightness of the TarraWarra Museum of Art have at last created a third field in the architecture domain of his city, a contribution that has brought the local architecture to its current high pitch – even if, for him, this continues to be at the cost of a concern that developing this degree of self-consciousness might lead to a loss of the impulse to create.

Firms That Sustain Innovation from Within

ARM

In the last 15 years, ARM has emerged as one of Australia's most successful innovative practices. Howard Raggatt[74] and Ian McDougall[75] completed the masters at RMIT at a crucial threshold in their establishment of their mastery platforms; Steve Ashton completed an MBA that has complemented these with a mastery of the processes in which 'the brain of the firm'[76] is nourished. From these bases they have launched and maintained a stream of architectural innovation that has transformed the way in which public architecture is conceived in Australia, and their work has attracted international scrutiny[77] and some notoriety (though this is incidental, arising from client programmes and not due to any 'larrikin' objectives). Their work is characterised by the thoroughness of the research they bring to bear on every project and their active listening to their clients, which engages those clients in furthering innovation in the interests of expressing their institutional goals. Initially concerned to limit the size of their practice to 20 people, they have seen it grow to a steady state of around 40 and are contemplating another tranche of expansion.

Meeting them together, I asked them what they had done to make their firm the powerhouse of innovation that it has persisted in being, where other practices that reach this scale so often run out of creative steam and concentrate on the pragmatics of the business, leaving design to recent graduates. They found the question difficult to answer head-on. Their architectural ambition looms large in their minds, and that vital concern for the domain as a discourse has in a sense governed their thinking about innovation. Thinking back through their operations over the years, they surfaced a number of significant practices that support their ambitions. Steve Ashton leads them through a business planning process that has from the outset concentrated on four goals. Firstly, the need to build 'regard and reputation' for the firm amongst their peers, locally and nationally. Recently the international dimension of this has become important to them, and they are poised to undertake significant work outside Australia. Secondly, the determination to do 'interesting work'. This has concentrated their efforts in the public realm, and began with a deliberate decision 'to do no more houses' – more on this decision later. Thirdly, they were concerned to have a good working environment, for themselves initially and later including the entire office. The importance of this aim has grown in their minds as time has passed. They are able to attract very talented and committed staff who 'like working there, and stay on'. Finally, they were determined to break the mould of the avant-garde 'starving in a garret' approach to innovation – they aimed to create a profitable business able to reinvest in developing its capabilities, sustaining an involvement in new technologies and nurturing staff.

As they talked through the question, it emerged that they embody in their practice many of the essential components for a successful learning community, or community of practice:

• It is a collection (collective) of willing individuals.

Bottom left
Howard Raggatt, an image from his masters, Fin de Siècle, 1993

Bottom right
ARM, RMIT Storey Hall, Melbourne, 1995
In creative terms, ARM is a mature collective. Its intellectual dynamic, formed when its three partners came together, is maintained through a conscious management process and is kept in disequilibrium by the allied but distinctive design approaches of Howard Raggatt and Ian McDougall.

These differences surfaced in their masters at RMIT. Raggatt pioneered new methods of design based on the noise in the machine – inevitable interferences with communication. McDougall filled out the notion of the need for public architecture to communicate with the public. Their buildings result from understanding the sense of stories imparted by their clients, their ability to find unexpected ways of meeting needs and managing expectations. RMIT Storey Hall projects the university's desire to be at the forefront of

technical education and research. The facade expresses the use of Roger Penrose's nonperiodic tiling, the system used to reclad the interior of the existing, neo-classical assembly hall. This skin incorporates air conditioning, acoustics and access systems. It is acknowledged as the first building in the world to use the new mathematics. The dynamic between the three partners continues to drive the firm into new creative innovations.

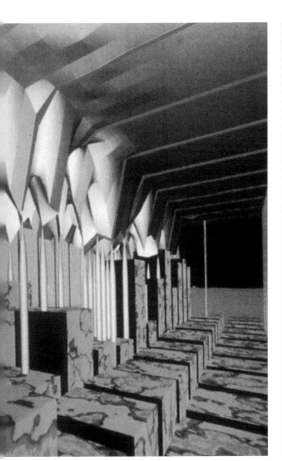

ARM, RMIT Storey Hall,
Melbourne, 1995

The partnership began in this way, and their office – quite informally – has built on this model of association. Their patent architectural ambitions attract certain kinds of people. In this sense they do not employ normative professionals, but advocates of their way of doing architecture. Their determination to embrace new technologies at the core of their practice also determines who wants to work with them.

• They have shared goals, a common vision and confront a similar sense of adversity in Australia's 'tyranny of distance'. As students they faced an education that they characterise as 'a social science course', and their determination to work for an architectural culture stems from this 'shared adversity'. Their early experience was all in practices committed to a social good, public works ethos. They became increasingly uncomfortable about single-house practice, which at best serves less than 3 per cent of the population and drives, they believe, the perception that architecture is a service only to elites.

• They have a shared leadership model. Committed to architecture as discourse, their leadership model is a discourse model. Argument is their medium and ideas win out on their merits. Everyone participates. They are interested in longevity in practice, not in the fireworks and momentary displays of individual fame. Theirs is a 'protestant' model of shared work and community, rather than individual glory.

• They subscribe to common processes, and have a shared sense of the rituals and rules of interaction that govern or should govern their practice behaviours. They do not have a standardised project review process, but do occasional 'show and tell' sessions and hold desk crits. They are careful about socialising staff into the office. Occasionally staff are invited to present 'their lives in five slides' to establish their personas in the office. They rent a beach house for the use of the staff. They employ enough staff to avoid the 16-hour working days that plague some small practices. They avoid retrenching in downturns.

• They have adopted strategies that make them capable of generating social capital – thus able to invest in continuing research and development. This they have done through a commitment to being in the forefront of the developing technologies but always in a gradual manner, avoiding big-bang roll-outs in favour of progressive renewal of the technical infrastructure. In this way they attract staff who want to be at the cutting edge, but avoid being overcapitalised around an ageing system.

Away from their own practice, they have committed to an active involvement in their community of practice, hosting in the office various publications by students and young practitioners and contributing to the development of the local chapter of the Institute of Architects (Steve and Ian have served as chapter presidents). Ian served as editor of the national institute's magazine for a few years. In these roles their aim has been to widen the reach of the peer-review processes of the

community through capturing and publishing local discourse, and extending the reach of the awards process. In the pursuit of continuing their researches, and the development of their arguments, Howard and Ian have taught at RMIT, latterly at postgraduate level. They see this as making a 'broad cultural and argumentative' contribution, as opposed to using the institutions self-interestedly as positioning opportunities. They have not developed a school of followers amongst their students, for example, but have assisted them in finding their own voices. In common with many of the new practices they do not 'market' themselves through networking, but rely on their research agenda to drive the work and attract clients. They have a strong circle of professional friends, with whom they can be very demanding because it is understood that they demand so much from their own projects. They are very open with these friends, discussing their fee levels, doing post mortems on competitions, often joining round-table discussions with them to debate the import of their various trajectories as designers.

There is in their discussion a broad sense in which they decline to see themselves as victims of history. Even if the plan is not explicit, they act as if it is possible to curate themselves into better, more appropriate situations. This is in itself a self-fulfilling prophecy. It is this that in part makes them such compelling leaders, not only in their practice, but also in the wider community of practice that they consciously seek to support through building

arguments, capturing local knowledge and supporting their peers in their endeavours where these further the ambitions of architecture. They see themselves as embedded in a culture, and look to work that has been 'panel-beaten' by that culture, work that is engaged.

The danger for this implicit approach lies in the possibility of its being unintentionally undermined, as it could be by their becoming embroiled in negative projects, such as building reputation through legal and quasi-legal routes (which happens all too often!), or giving way to the well-known innovation pitfall of 'founder's syndrome': the attempt to remain in control of invention to the consequently bitter end, another all too familiar situation in creative fields.

Lyons

Carey Lyon did the masters at RMIT,[78] defining an autonomous zone for architectural production in late capitalism in the 100-millimetre-deep skin of buildings. He was working as the project architect for an established firm of architects (Perrott Lyon Mathieson) on a major building in Melbourne: Telstra Headquarters. On completion of this building he formed an alliance with two of his brothers, Corbett and Cameron, to form Lyons, a practice that has developed an enviable reputation for design innovation in very lean fields – further education and health. This acceptance of the notion that the larger firm is a vehicle for creative innovation distinguishes this case study from the others. Where ARM set out believing that 'big is bad', Carey's work in defining a research direction around which a practice could be built was joined by Corbett's analogous postgraduate experience with the Venturis and Cameron's passion for technology. Their ready acceptance of the possibility of the firm as a vehicle for architecture of ambition meant that from its outset the firm involved younger architects in the development of its culture and today Neil Appleton and Adrian Stanic play a full part in the development of the firm's culture and help to ensure that its capabilities as a platform for innovation are maintained and grown. This inter-generational porosity has played a significant role in their continued vigour as a source of creative innovation in architecture. Neil Appleton completed a Masters in the Urban Architecture Laboratory programme at RMIT[79] after graduating from the undergraduate programme, establishing a substantial portfolio of works. Adrian Stanic is currently contemplating engaging in postgraduate design work.

I met with four of them to ask: 'What is it that you have done to create in your practice a "sustained attention" to architecture of ambition?'

They responded eagerly and vociferously, with no hesitation. Speaking in turn, and often completing each other's sentences, they outlined a series of deliberate strategies. When these are analysed, a clear model emerges, of which each one of them – 'jointly and severally' – considers himself a curator. You can visualise this model as a conical peak ringed by holding statements, framed by a series of evaluation events, backgrounded by a set of working strategies and with a skirt of attributes in the foothills. The model does not end as a landscape; this vista is framed by the personas of the players, each expressed through a series of individually defining moments:
- Carey's articulation of 'surface architecture' and the open question of what his next developmental quest will be.
- Corbett's strong engagement with the Venturis and an architecture of representation.
- Cameron's pursuit of technical solutions and materials innovation.
- Neil's fascination with the *Delirious New York* approach to understanding the continuities between popular culture and architecture.
- Adrian's seminal 'surface' major project as an undergraduate and his continuing search for

analogous works, in a study of Herzog and de Meuron, for example.

All of them pursue these interests in the laboratories of teaching in the universities.

These mutually defined personal trajectories overlook the peak. At its pinnacle it is inscribed (conceptually!) with the motto: 'The Idea of Architecture.' A contour below this is the unifying action statement: This practice is about 'pushing the idea'. They say: 'The word "idea" differentiates us. It brings us clients and projects that desire public resonance.' The interactions set up at this level of the model drive the implementation of 'sustained attention'. Behind are a series of triumphal arches, each recognising the establishment of a platform of mastery from which new innovations have been launched. The first was their exhibit 'City of Fiction', designed for the Seppelt Contemporary Design Awards (Museum of Contemporary Art, Sydney, 1999) in which featured their early ventures into a skinned architecture. These works had revolutionised the notion of the facade by working the 100-millimetre 'skin of architectural autonomy' internally and externally, thus winning for their clients large terrains of highly articulated internal space as well as signing the institutions public roles externally. The exhibition expressed this doubling of the facade (and the invention of new public space) by hanging hundreds of packs of cards printed with images of these built outcomes, playing the same magic. The exhibit won the people's award and took Lyons to Venice, where in 2000 they represented Australia. More importantly, it fully articulated the accomplishments of the first stage of their journey into innovation. In 2003 they undertook another major review of their progress, in what they describe as an 'End Stop Event'. Here they confronted their now well-established reputation for doing wonderful work within the leanest budgets in industry (government-funded education and health projects). They questioned the implications for future practice of their reputation as architects who could achieve well beyond their clients' initial expectations within an economy of means. They were concerned that this was becoming a formula, rather than an idea, and they challenged themselves with the task of finding new ways to accomplish as much while still pursuing the principle of parsimony. A second platform was defined; innovations are set to flow.

In the background of the model lies a set of organisational techniques that are employed to engage with clients. Lyons invariably 'workshop' their projects with clients, who enter into the design process and begin to look for areas in which to push the idea themselves. The design process is supported by regular interim office crits.

The attributes that they identify include a readiness to accept givens: 'We don't build resistance, we get quickly to the interesting ground with clients, who then begin to look for areas to push the idea themselves.' They work hard to 'find the ground where the idea of any project can be pushed', and build client and collaborator enthusiasm so that both tradesmen and Nobel Laureates take hold of the concepts and work with

them. Suspicious of formulas, especially ones they
form themselves, they term them 'defaults' and
challenge them deliberately. They ensure that each
project is a Research and Development project for
both technical and conceptual improvements. They
know what 'we don't want to do'. Projects in the
public realm, projects that need to engage with
society, are sought out. They see themselves as
'pushing representation, identifying areas that are
not challenging to us, identifying whom we want to
work for next.' Every project is treated like a
competition, giving every team 'the imprimatur to
radicalise every project to a degree'. They do this
because they pursue exciting ways to work in a
practice, keeping themselves creative even though
they work in building-type-driven areas.
Competitions are regularly undertaken,
acknowledging short-term exhaustion and the
longer-term building of energy. They equip the office
for 'digital depth', ensuring that they are working at
the cutting edges of the means of design and
production. And they have a shared interest in the
wider culture of their city, for example, collecting art
by artists whom they see as 'fellow travellers'.

Thwarted Mastery

How is it that so few of us reach our potential as innovators in practice? What is it that allows us to construct alibis of being too busy to focus on our ongoing development – even when we know in our hearts that our working lives would be better if we did allocate time to this? So many practitioners in their New Year resolutions set aside an afternoon a week to look, read and think, but all too frequently this or that crisis takes priority. So many practices try to meet on Friday evenings to discuss the work of their office in a reflective way, but enthusiasm for this tails off as those aspects of office politics that inhibit everyday discussion in other than an operative mode assert themselves with a vengeance. Why does this happen? Can we uncover the factors that inhibit continuous creative involvements with our work? What are the factors that thwart the transformation of our mastery into innovation? If identified, can they be challenged? Studies in other fields suggest that there are four main strands of thwarting:

• The overshadowing of a domain by a controlling master.
• A focus within a domain on technical refinement at the expense of other speculations.
• An amnesia about the cultural capital of a domain.
• Confusion about the knowledge base of a domain.

A fifth condition arises from the mastery/innovation distinction:
• A failure to elevate innovation out of the community that forged the platform of mastery from which it has sprung into a metropolitan discourse.

If we understand how these factors operate in our domain we can avoid the sad story of misdirected energy that is so often all that is left to be told at the end of another year. Perhaps we can change our office culture. Perhaps we can situate ourselves within a different external peer group. Many periods of intense creative productivity flow from rebellions against the thwarting of mastery, inside offices and in a domain, in a city region.

We are now familiar with the notion that for you to achieve a mastery that leads to creative innovation, you need to develop support structures, real and virtual, through your interactions with your peers and mentors. Unfortunately most mastery ends in competence rather than creative innovation. If we lived in a universe in which all was known that would perhaps not be a problem, but in a universe that is a learning organism, static competency soon ceases to be mastery. It fades into irrelevance. Even if you survive the twin temptations of stopping at mastery and concentrating on the maintenance of a tradition and an income stream, the shift from mastery to creative innovation can be thwarted by a twisted skein of other factors – forces that have been identified in operation through the centuries. While it is convenient to deal with these in separate sections, they are, it seems to me, not easily separable, one giving rise to the circumstances that promote the other.

Overshadowing: The Overshadowing of a Domain by a Controlling Master

All too often a domain comes to be dominated by one figure, in architecture usually someone who combines a charismatic design flair with a talent and enthusiasm for the politics of the institutions – formal and informal – that govern the discourse in a domain. Under such a regime, new ideas are dismissed as they emerge. Quite deliberately they are denied the sustained attention that they require if they are to become innovations that change the way in which we think in a domain. That is precisely why in an overshadowed domain there is a huge emphasis on what is legitimate and little relish for lively debate between the two or three poles of argument that exist in a vigorous intellectual climate. There are different kinds of overshadowing. Three kinds that impinge specifically on architecture as a domain at large are dysfunctional enchainment, foreclosing curatorial practices and prescriptive theorising. Overshadowing operates in different ways within large corporate firms, in smaller partnerships and within ateliers formed around one or two principals. As would-be innovators, we need to be conscious of these in the environments of our domain, our region and our workplace:

- Overshadowing through dysfunctional enchainment. Enchainment is crucial to our development, but choosing certain kinds of mentors and peers can lead to our mastery's being thwarted.
- Overshadowing through curation. Self-curation is the fundamental tool for developing mastery and transcending it. Yet we can become entangled in curatorial practices that deny that development. Most importantly, these include the procurement processes by which architecture is commissioned.
- Overshadowing through theory. This is perhaps the most insidious way in which our development can be thwarted. Theory seems to be automatically enabling, but much of it is intent on foreclosing on options rather than opening the way to further exploration.

Technical Over-refinement – A Focus Within a Domain on Technical Refinement at the Expense of Other Speculations

There is an ongoing debate about whether ideas lead to tools or tools give rise to ideas.[80] We can be sure that this is not a simple binary opposition, but domains in which the dominant emphasis is on technical refinement soon lose the capacity to innovate. Why then would a domain become focused on the refining of the technical? The answer is probably political. One of the main techniques of those seeking to control a domain is to limit the scope of what can properly be regarded as within that domain. Many forms of refinement can be promoted as a replacement for the pursuit of intellectual change. The famous phrase 'touching the ground lightly', uttered by Glenn Murcutt, an innovator in Mies's school, has given rise to a school of imitative architecture, which is thinly articulated around exploring this singular principle. This is a form of enchainment that must be disconcerting to its perpetrator, whose own works break this dictum as often as not.

Forgetting Cultural Capital

Forgetting cultural capital condemns a domain to chasing its own tail, reinventing the wheel, as we say. Why forget? Often this is an agreed amnesia because forgetting in these circumstances is seldom a matter of forgetfulness. Cultural capital is suppressed in one way or another, sometimes in a mutual compact between mentors and those seeking

Metropolis in the province, the province in the metropolis
The intense 18th-century urbanity of the small town of Wisbech in Cambridgeshire (top) speaks of a metropolitan cast of mind, and Primrose Hill in London (bottom) displays a coeval ideal of a picturesque villa in Arcadia, a dream of the provinces. These different aspirations show how – in the Age of Enlightenment – the metropolitan was a state of mind, not a geographical situation.

Page 157
Louis Kahn, Indian Institute
of Management, Ahmadabad,
India, 1962–74

mastery, sometimes by an overshadowing figure who rewrites history to secure a power position. Aggressive forgetting is a tool of curators who highlight one part of the canon at the expense of others. In some city-states the government architect has managed to enforce a curatorial orthodoxy on all government commissions, creating a chain of patronage that favours one school and, as often as not, one mentor.

Confusing the Knowledge Base

When we embark on a pursuit of mastery, and even more so when we seek to become innovators on a basis of mastery, our energies can be diverted into unproductive realms if we seek to establish our positions on a knowledge base that our domain does not command. This is not to argue against cross-pollination – far from it. We gain enormous energy from aligning the boundaries of our knowledge with the horizons of other knowledge areas. However, we can waste our energies defending our professional status against incursions from other practices when we choose to base our mastery on a knowledge base that is not at its core the stuff of our domain. Professions are practices based on the custody of a body of knowledge and exercised with a degree of autonomy on behalf of society at large. If the practice is centred on a body of knowledge that society does not regard as ours, then there is no autonomy, no profession. Architecture becomes professionalised around the notion of the 'master builder', rather than spatial intelligence[81] and this has diverted most institutional support for mastery into a doomed politics of exclusion that saps energy and denies the domain a focus on the ways in which architecture intersects with the lives of everyone.

Failing to Elevate Innovations into a Metropolitan Discourse

Loyalty to the local conditions that have given rise to an insight leading to an innovation can result in the failure of the realised innovation to become part of the best possible conversation in a domain. This tribal identification with the province that has given rise to the conditions can thwart the further development of innovation, just as a denial of the provincial or actual origins of innovation can turn it into a classicising, normative force. It is easy to confuse the issues at stake here:

provincial actualities exist throughout any geographical metropolis and metropolitan conditions surface in any region that finds connections to the widest web of the discourse of a domain. At the AA in 1986 I ran a unit with Alvin Boyarsky and Dalibor Vesely that set out to show that in the 18th century the town of Wisbech in Cambridgeshire had harboured metropolitan ideals of urbanism at a time when much of London was sunk in the survival-level conditions that are generally assumed to be of the periphery, or of the developing world. Alvin's famous suspicion of the countryside was set aside and he travelled to Wisbech to see for himself a microcosm of all that the Age of Enlightenment could imagine as 'metropolitan', all referenced to the medieval gloom of east London that Vesely's pioneering students had described. I have come to believe that Rafael Moneo's work, which is discussed later in this section, is wonderful because it is so much of its region. A sense that it is 'architecture' of a universal kind denies it the resistance of other places, and it can, as in my view at Davis Museum, Wellesley College, Massachusetts, sit uncomfortably in an alien context. Some critics sense the same failure when Alvaro Siza's sensibility is shifted from Portugal to the Netherlands. Has the translation worked? Alternatively, when a breakthrough is made in a city region and it languishes there, the danger exists that the innovation becomes captive to the locality and spirals into Mannerism (as Heinrich Wölfflin famously argued).[82]

Conclusion

Thwarted mastery is not a stable condition. While a local domain can be held in thrall for a very long time by people who are ruthless or litigious, such domination cannot be sustained. The law of small numbers has been derived from observing the way in which such uniform terrains become – inevitably – the locus for rebellion, if we are lucky, and revolution, if we are not. Lucky, because rebellion opens up to several new possibilities, including that which is being rebelled against. Unlucky, because one school has been replaced by another, as ruthlessly controlled by some former victims who have learnt all the tricks of repression.

Louis Kahn, Indian Institute of Management, Ahmadabad, India, 1962–74

The architecture of Louis Kahn is so complete in itself that rather than posing questions it demands replication. Something about his theoretical position, and the way in which he was cast as a great master to be revered, makes him a difficult mentor. In his philosophising and his design he seems to exhaust his proposition, leaving no room for further development, defying hybridisation. In the Indian Institute of Management at Ahmadabad, for example, his charismatic geometry seems to resonate profoundly with the ancient astrological instruments of Rajasthan. These axes, arcs and coils hold the scholarly life in a prescribed system that invites admiration and contemplation. But repeated, these forms give rise to dim resonances only.

Ludwig Mies van der Rohe, Illinois Institute of Technology, Chicago, 1956
While as powerful a figure as Wright or Kahn, Mies's even more hermetic-seeming pursuit of perfection actually has become a platform for further innovations by later generations. His abstract organising systems re-invigorated frame construction and opened up for many the pursuit of a perfect fit between structure, skin and a tight fit to programme.

positions, and they do not form around syntactic peculiarities. Formal structures seldom have this in mind. They are more concerned with regulating the relationships between their members, ironing out conflicts of interest, than they are in intellectual change. That is left to the universities, where other paradigms are at play (research in university contexts takes place in a completely separate field of play). For architecture this tends to leave innovation in the core practice without formal structures of support.

On the other hand, informal supportive structures are often quite properly ephemeral. Black Mountain College was an experiment in education that lived within the frame of a certain ideal of human difference and died when that was traduced. Maybe the best structures are consciously ephemeral, focused on an idea at a time. In the case studies I examine the efforts of people who have set out to establish peer-review processes: Peter Corrigan and Ian McDougall, and in another, gendered sense Dimity Reed in Melbourne, William Lim in Singapore and Asia, and Ken Yeang in a moment of new global optimism. All of these were prompted certainly by a determination that there be a mastery in the new post-colonial world, a world not dominated by the metropolis in the old imperial sense; but also, perhaps, they reach towards a mastery structure enabled by the metropolis in the new Internet world.

Overshadowing through Curation

Curatorial practice can close down innovation as

readily as it can open it up. There is a close link between this and patronage, as most patronage is influenced by a curatorial position. Philip Johnson is an architect who has used his influence to define a series of platforms for innovation. His influence has been exercised through the Museum of Modern Art (MOMA). 'This is Modern Architecture' (1932) was succeeded by 'Complexity and Contradiction' (1966) and then by 'Deconstruction' (1988). Each of these curatorial initiatives created vogues in patronage that both validated and directed the energies of architects for some years to come. There has been intense debate about whether these curatorial ventures have opened up patronage or whether they have circumscribed patronage to an anointed few. Many feel overshadowed and excluded by these canonical moves.

Conversely, Japanese architect Arata Isozaki has risen to a position in which he can influence many flows of patronage in Japan, and to a considerable extent he has used that influence to open up opportunities for unknown architects. His admiration for Alvin Boyarsky led him to turn his mind to helping a new generation of potentially innovative architects into positions in which their work could be built and thus become the subject of sustained scrutiny. His Osaka Follies project began this, and it continued with the Kumamoto Art Polis project. Even so, there are those who argue that he could have used his influence to promote a more comprehensive selection of creative beginners.

The curatorial process is more starkly evident in the art world, where a critic and gallery sales nexus

is clearly visible. Clement Greenberg used a prescriptive account of what was and was not Abstract Expressionism both to create a market for a certain kind of art and to ensure that there was a shortage of supply by tightly prescribing the origins of the work that was allowed into the canon. This was also a fight to replace Paris with New York as the fountainhead of innovation in art. Today, an open-ended and exploratory curatorial position has dislodged the exclusive and excluding machinations of the ANY decade, and Paris – by way of Archilab – has found a way ahead through an inclusive fascination with experimental architecture, wherever it is being pursued.

Overshadowing through Theory

Like mastery, the theorising of a domain can be based on the desire to open up to new understandings, or it can be a tool for insisting on the merits of an established golden age, eschewing innovation as a dilution or betrayal of that age. Darwin and Einstein were generous in establishing platforms for future exploration while Wallace and Poincaré tried to tie the future of their findings to the past. Architecture is complicated by a tension between forms of knowledge developed through spatial – and other – intelligence. In the ever-evolving universe, human capabilities are endlessly being extended by experience and learning. This means that our knowing is dynamic and changing, and it is fed by the experiences of everyone on the planet. Meanwhile the mastery of architecture is demonstrated through built artefacts and the diagrams that give them their facture, their intent. These artefacts are collected into a canon – if you are a golden-ager – or into a plurality of canons if you embrace the need to surf evolution's breaking wave.

There are many arguments used to close down innovation in favour of an assertion that architecture has been solved. There are also manoeuvres that turn an opening-out theory into a closing-down practice. Conrad Jameson[85] seems to hanker after a golden age of vernacular building in which place, process and people are enmeshed in an unselfconscious making of their world, rather like Bachelard's description of a robin,[86] making its nest round by pressing the rising layers of gathered strands into shape with its breast. Here the argument is that innovators betray the trust of the community by leading them into novelties that disrupt a previously existing harmony. This becomes a romantic argument against the division of labour and harks back to the medievalist passions of William Morris. In our current society, community activists – genuinely seeking to empower their clients – often connect them to an impoverished notion of what architecture is and what it can do, promoting a populist, nostalgic style. Thus an argument that radicalises the base of architectural knowledge, by widening it to include a custodial role for the spatial knowledge embedded in every human, becomes hostile to innovation, which is seen as an elite activity.

Classicists, on the other hand, hark back without discomfort to a more divided social model,

seeking to re-establish an age that read its own belief in the harmony and proportions of the universe into the ruins of antiquity. They assert that one or other part of the canon is the only socially desirable mode of architecture. Roger Scruton's praise for the civility of Georgian architecture conveniently ignores contemporary accounts of it, which show that dismay at the then new was as virulent as any current popular criticism of the now new. He also seems innocent of the class structure it was devised to protect, unaware that the Georgian town house was a carefully devised fortress, from its civil moats, railed with pointed stakes ('the area'), to its mob-proof front doors, fanlights and lobby.

But in both of these cases, the theorising has the same effect: it is used by those who wish to control the nature and scope of mastery in architecture. Some of these controllers are patrons with the power to commission large tracts of building. The curious relationship between Léon Krier and the Prince of Wales linked an educator who operated from a canonical position to a client with nostalgia for visual harmonies that seem to elude modern societies.[87] Krier would sit in his office at the Architectural Association, bottles of Tipp-Ex at hand, blotting out offending areas of student designs and redrawing them to suit the archetype that he and his brother Rob had generated from their experience of small European towns untouched by the consequences of industrialisation. This brings to mind another editing method: Gordon Cullen's improving erasures in the

Architectural Review in the 1960s, a tidying up that seemed innocent enough at the time but which, as we shall see, promoted a desire to ignore the forces at work in our cities.

Kenneth Frampton's tectonics[88] prescribe the ground rules of a 'modern' architecture that has solved all of its issues, and this prescription is intended to play out in schools of architecture. His *Critical Regionalism* was hailed as a liberating force in Australia, but it was the title that was seized upon, not the content. The book deals with the few permissible changes that could be wrought on the modernist canon through considerations of climates other than northern temperate. What could be critiqued was very circumscribed. In the famous clash between Frampton and Boyarsky in their late 1960s bids for the chairmanship of the Architectural Association School of Architecture, Frampton argued that there was no need for experiment, the canon of architecture was complete, and that education was a matter of a curriculum tightly defined to that canon. Boyarsky argued for experiment, later – legend has it – asserting as he lay dying, 'There will be no curriculum system at the AA!' Ironically, his pluralist position led him in his time to include in the AA many competing cuckoo-absolutists, each vying to throw the others out of the nest.

The nature of the restrictions that these forms of theorising lend themselves to becomes very apparent when you consider theories that expressly create platforms for innovation. Some of these feature in the next zone.

Technical Over-refinement

In my career the clearest examples of over-refinement thwarting architecture have come from a few areas of concern:

- Design methods
- Environmental sustainability
- System building
- Yachting

As will be immediately evident these are paradoxical situations. They are all incredibly well meant, benign in intention, and yet when practised in a blinkered and obsessive manner they thwart not only the possible architectural outcomes but also the narrow objectives that they espouse. Here I offer a thumbnail account of the intentions and the thwarting, with – where possible – an account of how the narrow focus has been transcended, and innovation has flowed.

Design Methods

This was a venture with admirable ambitions. Growing out of the systems-engineering approaches and successes of World War Two and the postwar reconstruction, and fuelled by the successes of the space race in the 1950s and 1960s, theorists imagined that if they could pin down a description of 'the' design process they could define an unfailing methodology for achieving successful architecture. Amongst these systems were Bonta's semiotic approach to an architectural language, espoused by the young Charles Jencks. Students laboured fruitlessly to design chess sets whose form

alone would communicate their function. Aligned with this approach, a notion of rational legibility coloured Christian Norberg-Schultz's prescriptive critical approach, an approach that could – alongside that of the hard-line modernist Kenneth Frampton – only observe in dismay what actually happened as architecture evolved in response to individual creative engagements with an evolving environment. Donald Schön's account of the reflective practitioner also became a prescription strangely divorced from the actualities of practice. Perhaps the most influential of these dead ends was Christopher Alexander's *Pattern Language*, which wonderfully recorded thousands of cases of lush situations – architecture without architects in the main – and suggested that design was a matter of assembling these around each new brief. Alas, these worthy combinations always seem to lack the architectural qualities that resonate with the inner knowledge of people – far better accounted for in Steen Eiler Rasmussen's open lattice account of architectural qualities.

Environmental Sustainability

Possibly, the record of environmentalists, whose efforts in influencing the design of buildings have been as successful as their efforts in influencing the design of motor cars, has been literally tragic. No amount of demonstration or exhortation seems able to lure people away from an almost bower-bird fascination with effects of shininess and slickness, of dazzle and lustre and blue. There have been moments when great theoreticians have seemed to

**Morris-Nunn & Associates,
Forest Eco Centre,
Scottsdale, Tasmania, 2002**
Perhaps the best way to
illustrate the effects of
technical over-refinement is to
describe a work that – thanks
to the wider intentions of the
architect – transcends all the
pitfalls of fascinations with
design methods,
environmental sustainability,
system building and yachting.
These bedevil almost
everyone who – for really
good reasons – becomes
involved in these worthy
enterprises. The Forest Eco
Centre in King Street,
Scottsdale, Tasmania,
designed by Robert Morris-
Nunn and Peter Walker of
Morris-Nunn & Associates, is
a building that partakes of all
these fascinations, and

Failing to Elevate Innovations into a Metropolitan Discourse

Rafael Moneo

Where innovations are trapped in the local, either because of a reluctance to subject them to self-conscious scrutiny or because their nature has been denied, a recursive cycle sets in, and the innovation either fails to develop or the practice itself becomes less able to modulate to new conditions.

This can happen even to people whose work we greatly admire and which has achieved widespread international recognition. My case study here is about the work of one of the acknowledged masters of the late 20th century. Doubts have begun to arise about the recent work, especially the cathedral in Los Angeles. I believe that this comes from the suppression of the local in this architect's account of his work in favour of a singular 'modernism' universally applicable. The case study is a first-person account of my discovery of the key to this puzzle. This is by no means a lost cause: recognition of the coexistence of different architectures along the lines of the law of small numbers would – I believe – dramatically alter the situation.

Reflections on the AA Asia visit to Spain, 23 December 1999

The last place we visited was El Escorial. Here for me everything, well, shall I say 'a lot', fell into place. Ever since I encountered Barcelona, I have marvelled at the particularity of its architectural culture. On this visit I had begun to be engaged with the equally vital, but equally particular architecture of Madrid. I wonder why this surprised me. Perhaps I felt that it was a little

unlikely for a country to have two such powerful traditions, and yet intellectually I knew that there was this dichotomy before I experienced it. Perhaps I can explain.

I first encountered Rafael Moneo, Josep Lluis Sert Professor of Architecture at the Graduate School of Design at Harvard, in action there in Boston in 1994. Obviously I had seen his work in illustration before that, and I enjoyed the easy lucidity of his debating style when he engaged with the labyrinth that seems to me to be Eisenman. But I became concerned that his view of architecture was restricting the educational exposure of students, even in the face of the possible contrary and exploratory influence of – in that semester – Zaha Hadid. One of my students, faced with the logic of a folded plate returned into a sharp triangle, wept with fear at the possible consequences of this departure from carefully articulated and modulated rectangular forms. Of course, there was a wider debate about 'rigour' that informed his panic. Moneo was its most visible peak; Wilfried Wang and others fleshed out the argument. But it did seem extraordinary to me that at a time when Mack Scogin was head of architecture, such attitudes could so strongly inform student expectations.

The logic of this architecture of minimum expression, least form and studied dynamic symmetry was in itself unexceptional. I began to take exception when Mohsen Mostafavi took me to see Moneo's Davis Museum at a college in the nearby hills. The founding buildings were neo-Tudor, with finely wrought brickwork and stone mullioned

Left
Francisco Cabrero and Rafael Aburto, Casa Sindical, 1949
'It is hard not to admire the rigour of the structural coordination of this complex building. The front of the building is massively gridded; the back exposes a curved staircase clad in glass block. The idea of a stripped classicism is filtered through the rationale of construction and subordinated to its urban site overlooking the Paseo del Prado.' *UIA International Architect Magazine*, Issue 2/1983.

Above
Rafael Moneo, Bankinter, Madrid, 1972–7

Left
Rafael Moneo, Atocha Railway Station, Madrid, 1992 (bombed 11 March 2004)
Insight is a first step towards innovation. When insight is projected unmediated by a dialogue between province and metropolis, the provincial can be asserted as a general condition. This happens in real estate perennially, with a confusion of symbol and actuality, and an uncritical acceptance of low-level congruence. Houses are advertised as Provencal or Tuscan, depending on a coat of paint and the application of

one characteristic detail. In serious architecture, the effects can be tragic. Moneo's amalgam of traditions from high Spain has created an architecture of rare power, able to strike levels and manipulate grids of facades in a lineage that stems from El Escorial and 1930s Rationalism. Bankinter in Madrid displays all the hallmarks of an innovation based on a deeply understood mastery of these precedents. So too does the railway station – a new ground plane has been created with all of the inevitability of the granite terrace at La Escorial. This new reality has an actuality that seems inevitable.

When it comes to buildings in the very different setting of Massachusetts, such as the Davis Center, these resonances are not available, and while the interior is compelling, the exterior seems to cry out for links back to EL Escorial, rather than to the Tudor fantasy of the college – a fantasy so strong that even Rudolph softens and moulds towards its silhouettes. If the compelling derivation of a regional, Madrid architecture had become the *modus operandi* for these new places, the architecture might have risen to further levels of innovation, rather than sticking to the already established plateau and its palette.

windows with many delicate, light-filled bays loosely articulated around incomplete quads. Paul Rudolph had completed one quad with a delicately responsive building that completely belied his Brutalist image. Tapering columns and carefully etiolated eaves spoke gently to the originals, and a series of levels ramped down to a lower level, creating the beginnings of a further quad down the hill. This Moneo's Davis Museum closes with a strikingly prismatic brick cuboid form, minimally penetrated with openings and top-lit. While the interior has a richly conceived double-stair circulation space and the galleries are spacious, the exterior seemed to me strangely out of place.

El Escorial gave the clue that convinced me that, despite the didactic insistence that his approach is generic, Moneo's architecture expresses a particular sense of place, a sense confined to Madrid and its region. His architecture is a response to a history of resistances specific to that culture, and perhaps to its qualities of light. To him this may be a weakness, to me it is the source of the 'wonder' (in Philip Fisher's sense – see last paragraph of this discussion) in his work. Anton Capitel, a Madrid-based architect and educator, showed us how the Federation of Workers' Union Building opposite the Prado was constructed according to Franco's requirement for classical symmetry. Two stone pavilions and a portico entrance face the avenue, making a show of classicism. Then the architect used a deep-set brick module as the frame for the offices behind, carefully proportioned with some evident awareness of the work of Terragni. This

180

brise-soleil crate deforms at the sides and at the back as the building adjusts to the form and the geography of the old city adjacent.

Capitel then showed us Moneo's Bankinter, further up the avenue. There is a similar virtuosity in arranging the building blocks relative to the pre-existing villa on the front of the site, and the wholesale adoption of the brick crate module and an immaculate adjustment of its proportions and scale to match this situation. In both cases the sharp rises and deep shadow lines play vigorously with the high dry light, and the orange of the brick seems to originate in the blue of the sky generated by this altitude.

Later we were shown the General Post Office and a hospital by Antonio Palacios, a 19th-century architect who developed a classicism of whole stone elements, with steel and glass bridges and airy conservatories.

At El Escorial, we discovered the brooding presence lying behind these buildings, a precedent that could not be ignored. This 14th-century masterpiece of austerity – spiritual and classical – strikes a level from the base of a foothill, and establishes a commanding terrace made real by huge stone flagstones to the formal north and east, and gravel and parterres to the south and west. Internally it is as if carved from rock. Whole granite slabs span the corridor floors. Columns are monolithic. Other surfaces are uniformly white-washed and edged in grey granite. A capacious but austere living quarter faces south, affording a distant view of Madrid. The grey granite of the

church is husk to a highly gilded altar screen, and nothing else is decorated. In contrast to the coldness of the living quarters, the crypt and its tombs are lavishly coloured and embossed with semiprecious stones.

As one looks at this, the salient skills of Moneo float into perspective: the matchless ability to strike a level and work through its logic so that it seems an event of nature rather than of human happenstance (see the railway station); the calculated limitation of materials; the scarcity and deliberated control of openings; the sharpness and the tendency to an orthogonal, underlying geometry.

Why deny it? Why suppress the history that it expresses? Why avoid the story of this architecture? There are reasons to argue against narrative in architecture. I like Philip Fisher's argument that at its best architecture evokes 'wonder' – a phenomenon in which the whole and its detail are grasped simultaneously. I agree that narrative surprise has been a failing strategy to import the immediate power of film into the medium of architecture. I agree that 'surprise' is not a good quality in architecture, though it is in narrative. But I fail to see how it can be argued that the detail does not include a history of the specific resistances of each city region and its own history of architectural endeavour. Moneo has so much more to teach us in this context than the fear of transgressing what becomes ironically a style when divorced from its particular enchainments.

Encouraging Mastery and Innovation

Just as there are distinctive ways in which our best ambitions can be thwarted – if we are not aware of them – there are environments that encourage such ambitions. With knowledge, these can be sought out and they can be created. In a nutshell, encouragement is about bringing 'sustained attention' to bear on our creative breakthroughs, so that, in time, they become 'innovations' – processes, services or products that travel all the way from being ideas to becoming realised actors in society. They become things that change the ways we think about a domain, and the ways we operate in a domain. Sustained attention environments are:

- Personal – like self-curation.
- Collective – like schools both formal (AA, RMIT) and informal as in 'the school of …'.
- Regional and provincial – as when project-procurement processes support local mastery and innovation.
- International, or rather 'metropolitan'.

Personal Environments That Encourage
How do we put ourselves in the position that we can give our own development the attention it needs if it is to benefit from our energies? Reinventing ourselves as the curators of our development is the crucial act – self-respecting and self-understanding curators, generous to ourselves and concerned always to open up options for others.

Studying the natural history of creative individuals, understanding what science has to tell us about our innate capabilities and how they unfold, we take command of our education and we direct it to support our abiding interests. We become connoisseurs of educational situations, learning how to pick and choose between them. Probably, taking advantage of the Internet, we become initiators of informal communities of learning that support us throughout our lives.

Studying the social practices of our domain, we situate ourselves in environments most likely to further our ability to express our ideas and test them. We seek out forums that engage with our interests, we publish in magazines, exhibit and invest our energies in cultivating certain conferences. We plan when and how to engage and at what stage.

By understanding the ways in which mastery is thwarted, we curate ourselves through difficult situations, with a more desirable environment in mind. Where overshadowing is unavoidable we seek out our own umbrellas; when attention is centred on one prevailing history we seek out that which is being forgotten.

We are particular about how we define our knowledge base, carefully defining ourselves to ourselves and to others. We choose our operating paradigm: are we in fact professionals, conforming to known prescribed norms of practice, or are we researchers in the modality of our domain, whose findings lead to a practice?

Collective Environments That Encourage

From time to time schools of architecture are consciously structured so as to promote the development of creative individuals. When this happens, they also help students to become self-curators within the embedded public behaviours of their communities of practice. As Aurelio Galfetti says: 'All we can hope to do is put them in the position of being architects!' Such schools emphasise the transformative journeys of learning rather than the curriculum. Occasionally groups of individuals cluster into schools intent on investigating the implications of an idea for their practice. For example, we have seen how three generations of Ticinese architects have explored ways of engaging their province with the wider ambitions of modernism. Such schools flourish when engaged in the open-ended thinking of generous theoreticians like Ignasi de Sola-Morales, people who discover something and say: 'Look at this. What could it mean for us?' Currently there is a tendency to focus on the creative collective. (Paul Carter's *Material Thinking* is a fascinating account of several such collaborations.)[95] This is a recognition that creativity transcends individual mastery and that innovation requires networks of support. Curators in the past have used the myth of the lone genius as a way of controlling markets. Such curators espoused a 'school' of purchasable creators, excluding, as did Clement Greenberg, anyone who deviated from their definition of collectible. Curator of architecture Frédéric Migayrou chose to work only with the experimental in architecture. In the absence of a market for such works, he emphasises nodes of metropolitan discourse that will determine future

The Architectural Association, London, 1847–

Founded 'by a pack of troublesome students' as a society for the promotion of self-education, self-reliance and learning, then becoming a school offering 'education for architects by architects', the Architectural Association was the English point of contact with CIAM (Congrès Internationaux d'Architecture Moderne) in the 1930s. It established the first school of tropical architecture in the world in 1953. In the late 1960s the Architectural Association School of Architecture elected to remain an independent institution outside the increasingly government-regulated university sector. Under the chairmanship of Alvin Boyarsky (1971–90) the school's reputation as the international centre for experimental architecture, developed under Diploma School leader Peter Cook, was fostered. Boyarsky's unique contribution was to understand the informal elements needed by a vibrant community of learning: a respect for all generations, the strong articulation of a few opposing positions in architecture, the curation of their discourse into exhibitions, publications, competitions and built works. Notable practitioners like Pritzker Prize-winner Zaha Hadid and many educators graduated from the Boyarsky years. See AA 74–75 History and Projects, Architectural Association (London), 1975.

Black Mountain College, North Carolina, USA 1933–56

Founded by dissident faculty and students from a humanities school in a university, Black Mountain College became a 'refuge or seedbed for some of the most singular literary and artistic talents of our time, including John Cage, Merce Cunningham, Charles Olson, Robert Creely, Josef Albers, Buckminster Fuller, Paul Goodman and Robert Rauschenberg. Situated in the foothills of North Carolina, it was an experiment in community that proved the forerunner of a wide range of innovations in art and education.' There were two distinct phases. In the late 1930s Walter Gropius lectured there and he and Marcel Breuer drew up plans for the college that were not realised. In the postwar period there was a flowering under the GI Bill, with an interest in the 'minimum house' – interestingly, this coincided with a Cage and Cunningham residency. There was a student revolt against an Architects Collaborative design for a dormitory, which was then rejected, providing evidence of the power of the student body. Perhaps the most significant lesson of the two phases of the community of practice at Black Mountain was its interdisciplinary form, or rather, its scorn for boundaries between disciplines. Its decline was value-based: incidents of behaviour or sexual preference created rifts in the community that its educational mission did not bridge. See Martin Duberman, *Black Mountain, an Exploration in Community*, Norton (New York/London), 1993 (originally published 1972).

RMIT Architecture, Melbourne, 1887–

Architecture was taught at RMIT from 1887, the year in which the Working Men's College was founded as a night school. The expectation was that there would be 200 enrolments in all its courses. In the event, 2000 students turned up, half of them women. The college was graduating women long before the traditional universities allowed them to study at all. This always radical and sometimes obstreperous tradition has persisted into the centrally accountable eras of the late 20th and early 21st centuries. From the outset architecture has been taught by notable practitioners, beginning with Harold Desbrowe-Annear in 1888. The school has often used an intense practical engagement with its industry to envelope advanced theoretical speculation. This continued when in 1975 Peter Corrigan joined the staff. The school partook of most international trends in architectural education, without leading innovation. It developed its distinctive international reputation through the flowering of its engagement with the local community of practice in the 1990s, a relationship that has created a unique relationship between practitioners who have been in practice for a decade and established a peer-recognised mastery that they then examine in a critical framework, speculating about future innovative practice through the medium of design itself. This practice-based research culture imbues the undergraduate experience. See 'Back to School', *Architectural Design,* vol 74, no 5, Sept/Oct 2004, and Granville Wilson, *Centenary History*, RMIT (Melbourne), 1987.

Archilab, Orléans, France, 2000–

Growing out of the regional fund for contemporary art (FRAC) initiative that rolled out across France in the 1990s, Archilab is a partnership between the FRAC at Orléans', the City of Orléans and the Central Region of France, along with the Ministry of Culture, which administers the FRAC programme. Under the initial leadership of Frédéric Migayrou, followed by Marie-Ange Brayer, the Orléans FRAC has become an important collector and exhibitor of experimental architecture. Archilab is an annual international conference in Orléans, intended as 'a showcase for the most innovative architectural research programmes'. Young architects from around the world meet to show their projects and participate in 'an unprecedented forum of discussions and meetings that focus ... on the challenges facing architecture today'. The conference, open to the public, is now an 'indispensable point of reference for architectural and cultural circles'. Archilab creates an annual community of discourse between practitioners, theorists, critics and curators in a forcing house of seminars and communal meals. It is an example of how an international community of interest can be forged when the standardising norms of professional bodies are bypassed and the focus is on a specific mode of practice. See Frédéric Migayrou and Marie-Ange Brayer, *Archilab: Radical Experiments in Global Architecture*, Thames and Hudson (London), 2001.

Regional and Provincial Environments That Encourage

Procurement processes can be constructed to encourage a vital local culture of architecture – the informal structures of which are the basis for the sustained attention that creativity needs in order to become innovation. London's Jubilee Line is an example of a commissioning process – run by an architect – that reinstated the city as a locus for the work of its own architects. While one of those selected was well beyond the need for such support and may have, in Rowan Moore's view, long since moved out of the realm of creative innovation into that of brand marketing, the other stations demonstrate to the world that the local culture is indeed a force in its own right.[99] There is a recognisable commonality of approach – even if along a gradient of continuity – that enables anyone to become a connoisseur of London's design culture.

By contrast, the process that Groningen, a small city in the north of the Netherlands, has set in train demonstrates much that is wrong with most attempts to enliven a culture through building procurement processes. Here a range of international stars have been given their opportunity to display their mastery, and they have done so – often to stunning effect, especially when the work is at the scale of Bernard Tschumi's pavilion in a park. However, the larger effect is not to create any sense

of Groningen as a city with a vibrant culture; rather, it is more as if it is a city that, lacking its own wildlife, has settled for a zoo of exotics. In miniature this is the mistake that most cities make. Until we broke the mould at RMIT with a commissioning process deliberately programmed to provide opportunities in the inner city for the best of the local architects, Melbourne's centre was dominated by shadowy works from the offices of international giants: an undistinguished IM Pei, a less well-wrought Kurokawa. It was as if there was a corporate curatorial programme that wanted to dimly resonate with the great buildings of Tokyo and New York. This 'me too' approach may have made corporate cousins around the globe comfortable, but of course it did nothing to further Melbourne's reputation as a hot spot in design culture.

Starting with Edmond and Corrigan's Building 8 and then with ARM's Storey Hall, and continuing with Allan Powell's Building 94, followed by buildings by Wood Marsh and John Wardle, with attempts at commissions from Thompson, Godsell and others, we transformed expectations in the city and made it the norm, rather than the exception, to employ such local innovators. Melbourne now has an unparalleled reputation for architectural innovation, as attested to in the Venice Biennale in 2002, when no other city

The full list of Jubilee Line Extension architects is as follows:
Westminster – Michael Hopkins & Partners;
Waterloo – Jubilee Line Extension Architects;
Southwark – MacCormac Jamieson Prichard;
London Bridge – Weston Williamson;
Bermondsey – Ian Ritchie;
Canada Water – Jubilee Line Extension Architects;
Canary Wharf – Foster & Partners;
North Greenwich – Alsop Lyall & Stormer Architects;
Canning Town – John McAslan & Partner;
West Ham – van Heyningen & Haward;
Stratford – Chris Wilkinson Architects.

The Jubilee Line stretches across London east–west. It is a rare example of an infrastructural project that was brought into being through political use of public architecture, and which in its own conception created a showcase for London's capabilities in architecture. Without the Millennium Dome project, the line might not

have been built. Now it links Westminster from the London Eye to Canary Wharf, London's vast new commercial centre, and out to Stratford and thus to Europe. Tory politician Michael Heseltine understood the need for a 'magnet' to get the project going; the involvement of architect Richard Rogers – labour peer – kept the idea alive. Even though the dome was considered a failure as an event, the politics of its millennial ambition were the trigger for this wonderful string of works by London architects, an act of patronage that has helped to reassert London's architectural culture.

Below left
Foster & Partners, Canary Wharf tube station, London

Below right
Ian Ritchie, Bermonsey tube station, London

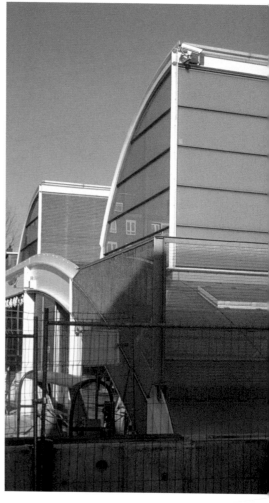

Below left
Jubilee Line Extension
Architects, Canada Water
tube station, London

Below right
Marks Barfield Architects,
The London Eye

was represented in every section of the Deyan Sudjic-curated Arsenale, and work from the city was present in other pavilions too.

Singapore and Barcelona are cities that share a strange circumstance. Both have had periods of intense local patronage, followed by a retreat into internationalism. In Singapore's case this happened soon after the first wave of development and it would take an extensive history to uncover how the early pioneers were slowly marginalised. It was partly due to the extent of their early success and partly through rivalries that did not lead to a sustained arena of attention for all of their works, but largely because one amongst their number obtained the power to commission for the state and chose to bring in outsiders rather than to allow his competitors to prove their ongoing mettle. Barcelona, after a world-inspiring process of urban invigoration following the passing of Franco's regime, fell victim to its own success. A new mayor is reputed to have reasoned: 'If we have done so well, how much better will we do if we employ world-famous architects?' There has followed a series of problematic and far from distinguished major projects that leave one wondering where the local culture went wrong. Success can lead to singular power, overshadowing and stasis. And then one waits for the next rebellion.

Curation is not often seen as an architectural problem and, as I have shown, it is more readily apparent at work in the art world. Clearly one can discern a curation process at work in Groningen. There is one at work at the Serpentine Gallery in London now, with buildings perhaps disconcertingly becoming as impermanent and as transient as sculptures. However, I would argue that there is a hidden curatorial practice at work in all educational institutions and in all commissioning. There are decisions made about employing people like us, or people whom people like us have employed, both in schools and in procurement processes. Unintended consequences arise in both instances when the overarching purpose is not properly argued through, is not stated and is unexamined. If there is one lesson from all of this, it is the need closely to examine what are the second order implications of decisions made to enchain yourself to one group or another, or to enchain, in a school or a procurement process, one group rather than another.

The star system that has characterised the passing of the postwar social contract between architects and the state is beginning to show the signs of its age, but for many the ANY series sought to define an in-group of architects motivated by the formal games that have enthralled Eisenman. It was not in any sense an inclusive model, and in his